FEEDING
FRIENDS

TERRY & GEORGE

FEEDING FRIENDS

PHOTOGRAPHY BY GEORGIE CLARKE
INSTAGRAM PHOTOGRAPHY BY TERRY & GEORGE
ILLUSTRATION BY WE THREE CLUB

HODDER &
STOUGHTON

This book is dedicated to our mums, two amazing women who are a massive part of who we are today and the food that we cook – we couldn't have done it without you! Cheers, Mum! xx

TERRY EDWARDS trained under the Michelin-starred chef Paul Heathcote in Liverpool before joining Michel Roux Jr. at Le Gavroche and then working with Mark Hix.

GEORGE CRAIG started the band One Night Only with a schoolfriend at the age of twelve. They made the top ten – and are still going strong today – but George has also developed a sideline in modelling, after he was scouted by Burberry.

Terry and George met through mutual friends. Terry introduced George to foodie London. George introduced Terry to the music scene. They soon realised they could combine their skills to put on pop-up restaurant nights mixing great food with amazing music – appealing to people who enjoy eating out with friends but who can't always afford full-blown 'fine dining'.

Inspired by British ingredients and culture, they have cooked sell-out nights in London, Manchester, New York and Hollywood.

CONTENTS

HELLO

Hello, we are the co-founders of **Check On** – a pop-up restaurant company focused on creating unique events. Imaginative yet unpretentious food is at the heart of our pop-ups, and bringing people together against the backdrop of a relaxed and friendly setting. In our first book, we want to share some of our favourite recipes with you and hope they inspire you to make incredible, exciting (and stress-free!) meals to feed your friends at home. Whether you want to go all out with a show-stopping beef Wellington or a simple yet tasty fish pie, we have it covered.

There is nothing better than gathering friends, family and loved ones together for a delicious meal. Food trends will come and go, but breaking bread with your nearest and dearest won't.

We don't want to get too mushy here but sod it, here goes…

For us, memories make great dishes and it's our memories that have inspired every single recipe in this book. What we hope is that the meals you create from these recipes will make new memories for you. Sharing a meal together is a simple act, but one that is so powerful it can comfort, heal, restore, excite, delight and surprise us and – most importantly – put a smile on your face.

Terry   *George*

HOW IT ALL BEGAN…

TERRY: After leaving school at sixteen I began working in pubs and bars. I didn't really know what I wanted to do career-wise but there was something about cooking programmes that had always intrigued me from a young age. While my mates were playing the latest Nintendo games, I was transfixed by Keith Floyd cooking up a paella or Marco Pierre White showing how to create the perfect pasta. Keith, Gordon, Marco – these were my heroes (not forgetting Everton FC's legends Neville Southall and Duncan Ferguson) growing up. As soon as I decided I wanted to get into cooking professionally, I never looked back. I've been living and breathing food ever since.

I first met George in a sticky-floored music venue in York around 2009. I had a week off from working for Paul (Heathcote) and was helping out on tour with a friend's band. George was back home in Yorkshire taking a break from recording his second album in Brussels. We didn't talk much that night, we just had a few drinks after the gig. Fast forward nine months and we'd both moved to London and started hanging out. I was working at HIX and George was just about to release his second album with One Night Only.

We'd eat out once or twice a week with friends on my nights off from the restaurant. This was all around the time that amazing pop-ups, supper clubs and, in fact, the whole street food revolution was just starting to really emerge. It was an exciting time, particularly as up until this point, you often had to spend quite a bit to get what all the 'foodies' were talking about. Now everyone, including the younger generation, had access to incredible food at affordable prices.

I remember George and I going to Broadway Market in East London and picking up a delicious, quality beefburger for a fiver – little more than your average takeaway meal deal but so much more satisfying!

GEORGE: My mum is an incredible cook and there was always a delicious roast or pie in the oven; I enjoyed eating a good meal but in terms of cooking one myself – I didn't know where to start! When the band and I started touring, I lived on junk food – it was a case of food as fuel to keep me going.

I started hanging out with Terry at his place and he casually got me involved with cooking. It was a very organic process; he never said, 'Right, George, today I'm going to teach you how to fillet a piece of fish.' I do remember the first night we cooked together for some friends. We made these awesome short rib beefburgers with tarragon mayonnaise, crispy bacon, iceberg lettuce, sweet potato fries and green tomato ketchup and they went down a treat. I put some

classic American vinyl on the record player and started to make some of our nutty White Russians. That was really the night that Check On was born. We were talking about how a lot of people will just get a case of beer and a couple of pizzas and leave it at that. Let's be honest: it's lazy and bad for you (I should know, I'd done it myself plenty of times).

We like to think we know how to put on a great party where everyone leaves happy, full and tipsy. I was running a club night in Camden at the time and Terry made these wicked Jack Daniels mince pies and a great spiced mulled cider for the Christmas party... people went crazy for them. It was a great night but it was the reaction to the food that was mind-blowing, especially

as people kept coming up to ask where they could sample more of our food. We realised then that we really wanted to start doing pop-up events.

Trying new things with Terry, like making fresh pasta or learning to cook a perfect steak, just made me want to taste more, eat more and eventually cook more. Terry taught me the importance of quality

ingredients and also that great food can be fun and imaginative without being intimidating. That's the ethos we bring to every Check On event and what we want to share with you in this book.

When I think back to the kind of food I was eating on the first tour with the band I can't believe how much has changed. Now, whenever we are in the recording studio

together, I'm always the designated chef and… I love it. I'll cook up a big stew or treat the lads to a beef Wellington. It's not just about the food. We'll all sit round the table together, switch off from work and relax. For me, the biggest buzz in cooking a meal for friends or family, is seeing them enjoy themselves and eating our food. That will never get old.

WHAT'S IT ALL ABOUT?

We have so much fun cooking together. We're constantly bouncing ideas off each other and know that in many homes, it's not always just one person doing the cooking for everyone else. Everyone chips in and helps and the kitchen becomes the place to hang out, listen to music over a glass of wine and catch up while peeling the spuds or getting the chicken in the oven. We've always tried to capture this relaxed, fun approach in our pop-up events and it's what we hope you'll find is at the heart of this book.

The book is divided into themes, from Comfort Food for long dark rainy days when only a steaming bowl of ham hock soup with crackling will hit the spot, to Great British Classics, where you'll find quality British ingredients such as pork and rhubarb paired together. A Very British Barbecue (drizzly rain and all), includes a great recipe for pineapple marinated in rum with a toffee sauce AND a prawn burger (officially our new obsession).

Other sections include Vegucation, where beautiful ingredients such as rainbow chard and even the humble cauliflower and onion are each given starring roles. We've also got a Leftovers section, drawing on ingredients used for other dishes in the book and showing how you can breathe life into them to create a whole new exciting dish. For us, eating well is all about balance and using quality ingredients.

We've tried hard to ensure that all the recipes are simple to follow, without lengthy lists of ingredients that will cost the earth. There are also plenty of sharing-style dishes where it's a case of bringing it to the table with a big spoon and letting friends and family tuck in. You can pick and choose dishes from across the sections to create the perfect menu. Our mission in this book is to take the stress out of cooking for you. We want to show you how easy it is to put together a lovely meal to share with your friends, whatever the occasion; whether it's a few mates crashing out in front of the telly, Sunday lunch for the family or feeding a crowd for a Christmas party.

We know from our pop-up events that a bit of careful planning goes a LONG way. While catering for 70 covers is quite different to an intimate gathering of friends, there are some general principles that still apply, and planning is most definitely one of them! A carefully thought-out menu and prepping as much in advance as possible can make the difference between you being able to enjoy the evening with your guests, and being glued to the stove the entire evening. And it's not JUST about the food… A cracking cocktail to greet your guests when they arrive always sets up the atmosphere for the evening

nicely. We've included a no-fuss drinks recipe in every section to get you started!

We want to share with you all the tips and tricks we've learnt along the way – the little details that make a big difference – such as lighting the room. Lighting a few candles is lovely if you're making a romantic meal for two, but string up some fairy lights to make it brighter for a bigger crowd.

A big part of what we feel has struck a chord with so many people who've come along to our pop-ups is the music playlists we create

for each one. Music is a massive part of our lives. It brings people together, gets them talking and is often a great ice-breaker. At the end of each section you'll find a playlist (you can also access these online; you'll find the link at checkonpresents.co.uk). We always have a record on when we're cooking. You can't beat a bit of The Beatles or Thin Lizzy playing in the background while you're chopping the veg!

Right, on to the first chapter. We're going to take you up North, to our first ever pop-up and for some classic comfort food!

GREEN PEA AND HAM HOCK SOUP WITH CRACKLING CRUMBS

BLACK PUDDING HASH WITH POACHED EGGS

SHELLFISH AND CHIPS WITH MUSHY PEAS

FISH PIE

LANCASHIRE HOT POT WITH BABY BEETS

TOAD IN THE HOLE WITH RED ONION GRAVY

EVIE'S YORKSHIRE PARKIN WITH SEA SALT CARAMEL

BAKEWELL TART

YORKSHIRE RHUBARB MARTINI

This opening chapter revisits the comfort food and dishes of our childhood – the places we grew up in and the friends we grew up with. Whether eating a bowl of soup with your sister on the sofa watching telly, fighting with the family over the sausages in the toad in the hole, or tucking into Friday night fish and chips. Comfort Food is universal – we each have our personal favourites, whether it's a steaming bowl of pasta covered in melted cheese on a miserable Monday evening or a plate of eggs the way you had them as a kid. For us, the best memories are the tastiest ones and the recipes here are all about relaxed eating.

POP-UP EVENT
NORTHERN INVASION

WHY NOT TRY...

Whether you're feeding five friends or 15, making them feel comfortable and relaxed is just as important as the food. We always leave a stack of records out and invite friends to get stuck in and choose the music. It instantly makes people feel at home. Whether you've got a CD player or iPod – it doesn't matter what – give your guests free rein to choose some tunes.

We were just two Northerners eating and cooking the food that we loved. So, we decided to go back to our roots for our first ever pop-up event and bring the food and music that we grew up with down to London, giving it our own twist.

TERRY: We started talking about the dishes we grew up with, such as the regular Friday fish supper that my mum would send me to collect from the chippy when I was a kid, and George's mum's famous toad in the hole that she would make on a Monday with her leftover Yorkshire pudding batter from the Sunday roast. Then there were the desserts such as Bakewell tart with ice cream and sticky, spicy Yorkshire parkin, which always hit the spot on a cold winter's evening. The menu came together really quickly.

GEORGE: The Northern Invasion pop-up was my very first night in the kitchen. I'll never forget burning the first batch of Bakewell tarts and thinking, 'What have I got myself into?' All our friends and family came to the first night and by the end of the evening my mum was in the kitchen, elbow deep in dishes in her posh frock. Everyone loved our food; they were really excited by what we were doing. It was a completely different experience from standing on stage at a gig in front of a huge crowd but it was equally as thrilling and I couldn't wait to do it all again the next night.

To set the relaxed and informal atmosphere of our first pop-up, we created a playlist featuring all the Northern music we both loved and had grown up with, including our musical heroes – The Stone Roses, Oasis and The La's, which we played during the pop-up. We also wanted to celebrate great Northern food and regional ingredients, such as Bury black pudding, Ginger Pig sausages and Yorkshire rhubarb, all of which featured on our Northern Invasion menu and so now are in the recipes we're about to share with you.

You can find a link to this playlist at
checkonpresents.co.uk

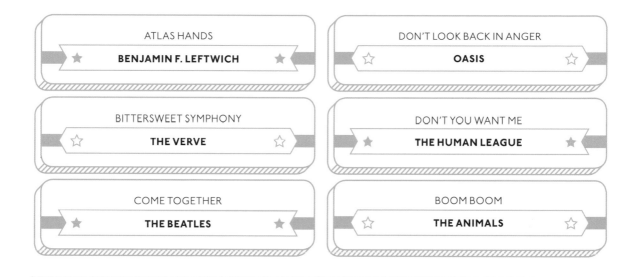

ATLAS HANDS
BENJAMIN F. LEFTWICH

DON'T LOOK BACK IN ANGER
OASIS

BITTERSWEET SYMPHONY
THE VERVE

DON'T YOU WANT ME
THE HUMAN LEAGUE

COME TOGETHER
THE BEATLES

BOOM BOOM
THE ANIMALS

PLAYLIST

DREAMING OF YOU
THE CORAL

VALERIE
THE ZUTONS

JUST FOR TONIGHT
ONE NIGHT ONLY

THERE SHE GOES
THE LA'S

I WANNA BE ADORED
THE STONE ROSES

LOVE WILL TEAR US APART
JOY DIVISION

GREEN PEA AND HAM HOCK SOUP WITH CRACKLING CRUMBS

This is a great and inexpensive hearty soup for a winter's evening. Everyone's got a bag of frozen peas in the freezer and this is the perfect way to use them up. The sweet pea and salt of the ham plus the texture of the crackling is the perfect combination. You can get a ham hock from your local butchers.

SERVES 6–8

100g butter
1 onion, diced
10 fresh mint leaves
1kg frozen peas
Sea salt and freshly ground
    black pepper

For the stock
1 ham hock
1 carrot
1 onion
1 bay leaf

1. First make the stock. Place the ham hock in a large pan with the carrot, onion and bay leaf and cover with 3 litres of cold water. Bring to the boil and simmer for 2–3 hours, or until the meat falls from the bone under its own weight. Check from time to time and top up with water as necessary so that the meat is always covered. Remove the ham hock and place to one side to cool. Strain the liquid, discarding the vegetables, and set aside.

2. Once the ham is cool enough to handle, remove the skin and meat from the bone and discard the bone. Flake the meat into small bite-sized pieces and set aside in a bowl until ready to serve.

3. Preheat the oven to 200°C/Gas 6.

4. Place on a baking tray. Sprinkle with sea salt and cook in the oven for about 25–30 minutes, or until completely crispy. Remove from the oven and place in a colander to cool and allow any excess fat to drain away. Once cooled, chop to a crumble consistency.

5. Melt the butter in a heavy-based pan and cook the chopped onion over a low heat, until soft and translucent.

6. Add the mint, frozen peas and 2 litres of the reserved ham stock to the pan and bring to the boil. Remove from the heat and leave to cool for 10 minutes before blending to a smooth silky soup with a hand-held stick blender. Season to taste with salt and pepper and then return to the pan to reheat gently.

7. Place about 50g of the flaked ham hock into each warm soup bowl and cover with the piping hot soup. Finish with a generous sprinkle of the crackling crumbs and serve immediately.

BLACK PUDDING HASH WITH POACHED EGGS

This is a great brunch dish and an alternative to the classic bubble and squeak. Get the best black pudding you can, as it makes all the difference – plus a couple of extra eggs. Whenever we make this we usually manage to break a few but nothing compares to the pride of poaching the perfect egg!

SERVES 4

Splash of white wine vinegar
8 free-range eggs
100g butter
1 onion, thinly sliced
2 garlic cloves, chopped
4 medium Maris Piper potatoes, peeled and diced
400g good-quality black pudding, diced
Splash of Worcestershire sauce
2 tbsp chopped parsley
Smoky Ketchup (see page 47), to serve

1. First poach the eggs. Bring a large, deep-sided pan of water to the boil and add a generous splash of white wine vinegar. Crack the eggs into small ramekins or cups and, once the water is at a rolling boil, slide them into the water. Cook the eggs in two batches for 3 minutes before removing from the pan with a slotted spoon and transferring to a bowl of iced water (this will stop the cooking process). Repeat with the remaining eggs and keep to one side until ready to serve.

2. Melt the butter in a large, heavy-based pan and soften the sliced onion and garlic over a low heat until soft and translucent.

3. Meanwhile, parboil the diced potatoes in salted boiling water until a knife glides through easily but they are still firm; drain and set aside.

4. Turn up the heat on the onions, add the diced black pudding and potatoes and cook until warmed through. Add a few splashes of Worcestershire sauce and the chopped parsley and fry for a few minutes, stirring with a wooden spoon.

5. Reheat your eggs in boiling water for 1 minute, then remove with a slotted spoon and serve on top of the piping-hot hash. Serve with Smoky Ketchup.

SHELLFISH AND CHIPS WITH MUSHY PEAS

Lets face it; we all love fish and chips! Here's our version, replacing the usual white fish with sweet scallops and crunchy crisp-like chips. You could serve these as individual portions in the scallop shells as a starter. The recipe here serves four as a main course.

SERVES 4

250g self-raising flour, plus extra for dusting
1 x 330ml bottle pale ale
50g butter
1 shallot, finely diced
500g frozen peas, thawed
5 fresh mint leaves
2 large Maris Piper potatoes, peeled and cut into thin matchsticks
2 litres sunflower oil
16 large scallops, cleaned and pink roe removed (see scallop salt, right)
Salt and freshly ground black pepper

1. First make the batter. Sift the flour into a large bowl and whisk in the beer (you may not need the whole bottle) until you have a thick consistency. Set aside.

2. Melt the butter in a pan and cook the shallot until soft and translucent. Add the peas, mint leaves and a splash of water and heat through for a couple of minutes before transferring to a food processor. Pulse briefly until you have a coarse 'mushy pea' consistency. Season to taste and set aside.

3. Wash the matchstick fries in a bowl of cold water to remove some of the starch. Drain thoroughly in a colander, then pat dry with a clean tea towel.

4. Heat the oil in a large, heavy-based pan with deep sides to 180°C – you can test if the oil is hot enough by dropping one chip into the oil: it should start bubbling immediately. Cook the fries (in batches if necessary) until they are crisp and golden. Remove from the pan and drain on kitchen paper to absorb any excess oil.

5. Dust the scallops in seasoned flour then coat in the beer batter. Reheat the oil that you used for the fries, then carefully drop the battered scallops into the hot oil and fry until golden, about 5 minutes. Cook in batches of five or six and place on kitchen paper to absorb any excess oil.

6. Reheat the pea purée and spoon on to warm plates. Place four scallops on top of each plate and scatter the fries over the top.

SCALLOP SALT

The scallop roe (sometimes also called the 'coral') is fine to eat but has a slightly bitter taste and usually cooks more quickly than the rest of the scallop. Use it instead to make scallop salt – a great seasoning for matchstick fries and fish. Preheat the oven to 100°C/Gas ¼. Place the roe on a baking tray and cook in the oven overnight until completely dehydrated. Tip the dried roe into a food processor with 250g good-quality sea salt and blitz until you have a powder-like consistency. Store in an airtight container for up to 3 months.

FISH PIE

There's something about fish pie that always tastes better when it's cold and rainy outside. There's nothing better than dishing this up to friends and family, straight from the oven to the table, bubbling at the edges. Definitely one to get stuck into! Our version is extra special, as we include egg yolks in the mash.

SERVES 6

30g butter
30g plain flour
350ml fish stock
200ml double cream
1 tsp English mustard
300g skinless smoked haddock
    fillet, cut into chunks
300g skinless salmon fillet,
    cut into chunks
300g raw peeled prawns
100g frozen peas
100g grated Cheddar
Salt and freshly ground
    black pepper

For the topping
5 large Maris Piper potatoes,
    peeled and diced
50ml hot milk
100g cold butter, diced
3 egg yolks

1. Preheat the oven to 180°C/Gas 4.

2. Melt the butter in a heavy-based pan and add the flour, whisking thoroughly. Cook for a minute or two, then gradually add the stock, whisking continuously to break up any lumps. Whisk in the double cream and mustard and bring to the boil. Season to taste with salt and pepper.

3. Add the fish and prawns to the creamy sauce, remove from the heat and gently stir together. Transfer to a large casserole dish and allow to cool for about 15 minutes before sprinkling with the peas and grated Cheddar.

4. Meanwhile prepare the topping. Place the diced potatoes in a pan of salted water and cook until tender; drain thoroughly and mash. While the potato mix is still hot, gradually add the milk and butter, beating until smooth. Once the butter and milk have been incorporated, add the yolks and season to taste.

5. Top the fish mix with the warm mashed potato and bake for 20–25 minutes, until golden and bubbling.

6. Serve 'family style' with one large spoon in the middle of the table, with some buttered green vegetables or a fresh green salad.

LANCASHIRE HOT POT WITH BABY BEETS

It doesn't really get more Northern than Lancashire hot pot. It's the ultimate one-pot wonder. In our version we add some baby beets, which gives a lovely rich, earthy gravy. You'll definitely want to bring out some sliced white bread to mop up the juices at the end.

TERRY: Every time I see it on a menu, I'm automatically drawn to it. It just reminds me of family meals and fighting over the crispy potatoes.

SERVES 4–6

1 tbsp flour
1 tsp sugar
700g diced lamb
   or mutton shoulder
1–2 tbsp vegetable oil
2 onions, sliced
3 carrots, roughly chopped
200–300g bunch of baby
   beetroot, peeled and halved
   (keep the tops)
1 tsp fresh thyme leaves
3 large Maris Piper potatoes,
   peeled and thinly sliced
600ml lamb stock
50g butter
Salt and freshly ground
   black pepper

1. Preheat the oven to 170°C/Gas 3.

2. Stir together the flour, sugar and a pinch of salt and pepper and use to coat the diced lamb or mutton.

3. Heat the oil in a heavy-based, deep casserole dish (with a lid) and brown the lamb or mutton, in batches if necessary. Return all the meat to the pan and add the sliced onions, carrots, beetroot and the thyme leaves. Generously season with salt and pepper and mix well.

4. Arrange the sliced potatoes on top of the meat and vegetable mix. Take care to make the potato layer nice and neat. Pour over just enough stock to come up to the bottom of the potato layer. Cover with the lid and bake in the oven for about 1½ hours (add 30 minutes to the cooking time if you are using mutton). Remove the lid and return to the oven for a further 30 minutes to crisp the potatoes.

5. Wash the beetroot tops, wilt in the butter with a good pinch of freshly ground black pepper and serve on the side. And don't forget the sliced white to mop up the juices!

TOAD IN THE HOLE
WITH RED ONION GRAVY

A dish that instantly takes us back to childhood... school dinners and family suppers. You can use leftover Yorkshire pudding batter from Sunday's roast to make this hearty meal.

GEORGE: Whatever you do, make sure you put enough sausages in. You don't want anyone to feel short-changed.

SERVES 4

200ml vegetable oil
12 large good-quality sausages
50g butter
3 large red onions, thinly sliced
2 garlic cloves, chopped
Pinch of fresh thyme leaves
1 tbsp flour
500ml beef stock
Salt and freshly ground
   black pepper

For the batter
300g plain flour
6 eggs
400ml milk

1. Preheat the oven to 200°C/Gas 6.

2. First make the batter. Tip the flour into a large bowl and make a well in the centre. Add the eggs and start whisking, adding the milk in a steady stream until you have a smooth batter. Set aside until you are ready to use.

3. Pour the vegetable oil into a large, deep-sided roasting tin to come about 1cm up the sides. Place in the oven for a few minutes to heat up.

4. Carefully remove the roasting tin and add the sausages, taking care not to splash any hot oil. Pour in the batter and return to the hot oven for 20–30 minutes, or until the batter is crisp and brown. Do not open the oven door for the first 20 minutes of the cooking time, otherwise the batter will sink.

5. Meanwhile make the gravy. Melt the butter in a pan over a low-medium heat and fry the onions, garlic and thyme leaves until softened, about 10 minutes. Stir in the flour and cook for 1–2 minutes. Add the beef stock and bring to the boil, allowing the gravy to thicken. Season to taste with salt and pepper.

6. Serve the toad in the hole straight from the oven, with a generous amount of onion gravy and some garden peas on the side.

EVIE'S YORKSHIRE PARKIN WITH SEA SALT CARAMEL

Yorkshire parkin is a cake traditionally made for Bonfire Night to celebrate Guy Fawkes. This cake gets better (and deliciously stickier) with age, and will last for around 2 weeks stored in an airtight container.

GEORGE: This is my Gran's recipe and when Terry was up in Yorkshire with me she made it for us. Terry loved it so much he made it back in London, adding a Check On twist with the sea salt caramel.

SERVES 4

200g butter
250g golden syrup
Juice of ½ orange
100g treacle
80g soft brown sugar
250g rolled jumbo oats
250g self-raising flour
1 tbsp ground ginger
Zest of 1 large orange
1 egg
20ml milk

For the caramel
300ml double cream
90g butter
120g light muscovado sugar
½ tsp sea salt, or to taste

1. Preheat the oven to 160°C/Gas 3 and line and grease a 22cm cake tin.

2. Place the butter, golden syrup, orange juice, treacle and sugar in a pan and gently warm over a low heat until melted and smooth.

3. Mix together the oats, flour, ginger and orange zest in a large bowl and slowly add the warm treacle mixture. Stir together the egg and milk in a separate bowl, then add to the parkin mixture and mix together.

4. Carefully pour the cake mixture into the prepared tin and bake for about 1 hour, or until firm and a knife inserted in the centre of the cake comes away clean. Remove from the oven, leave in the tin for a few minutes, then turn onto a wire rack to cool completely.

5. While the cake is cooling, make the caramel. Put the cream, butter and sugar in a heavy-based pan and place over a medium heat. Bring to the boil, whisking until the sauce thickens. Remove from the heat and add the sea salt to taste.

6. Cut the cake into squares and serve with the caramel sauce. It's nice and simple but super tasty. Perfect with a cuppa.

BAKEWELL TART

We're pretty sure everyone's introduction to a Bakewell tart was via a certain Mr Kipling, right? Try our recipe warm with ice cream.

SERVES 8

115g butter
115g caster sugar
2 eggs, beaten
120g ground almonds
20g plain flour
½ tsp baking powder
3 tbsp good-quality
    raspberry jam
Handful of flaked almonds,
    toasted, to serve

For the pastry
190g plain flour, plus extra
    for dusting
Pinch of sugar
85g chilled butter, plus extra
    for greasing

1. First make the pastry. Mix the flour and sugar in a bowl, then grate in the butter. Rub the butter into the flour with your fingertips until the mixture resembles fine breadcrumbs. Stir in just enough cold water to bring the mixture together into a smooth dough; it shouldn't be sticky. Wrap in cling film and chill for at least 1 hour.

2. Preheat the oven to 170°C/Gas 3 and lightly butter a 23cm loose-bottomed tart tin. Roll out the pastry on a lightly floured surface until it is about 3mm thick and large enough to line the tin. Line the tin with the pastry, easing it into the corners, then trim the edges. Line the pastry with baking paper and baking beans or dried pulses.

3. Bake blind in the oven for about 15 minutes, until the edges start to colour. Remove the paper and beans and return to the oven to cook for a further 10 minutes. Remove from the oven and allow to cool.

4. Meanwhile prepare the frangipane filling. Cream together the butter and sugar until pale and fluffy, either in a food processor or in a large bowl with a wooden spoon, then gradually add the beaten eggs. Fold in the ground almonds, flour and baking powder and combine until smooth.

5. Once the pastry base has cooled, spread the jam across the base followed by the frangipane mixture. Return to the oven to bake for 25 minutes, or until firm to the touch.

6. Allow to cool slightly before scattering some toasted almonds on top and cutting into slices. Serve warm, with clotted cream or vanilla ice cream.

YORKSHIRE RHUBARB MARTINI

Yorkshire is famous for rhubarb. It has a lovely almost sherbet flavour. This flavoured vodka is incredible and the hardest part is not drinking it while you wait for it to infuse! This is super simple to make – it's a case of whack it in and wait. We first started experimenting with infusing alcohol a few years back and it's become a staple of our pop-up dinners – we always finish with some free alcohol for our guests. Our motto is, if you leave drunk, you leave happy.

MAKES 1.3 LITRES

600g Yorkshire rhubarb, washed
   and cut into 2cm pieces
50ml grenadine
200g caster sugar
300ml water
650ml vodka

To serve
½ egg white
Ice

1. Place all the ingredients in a large airtight 2-litre container and leave to infuse for at least 4 days. Give it a good shake every day.

2. After 4 days strain the liquid through a sieve (or slowly through a fine cloth if you want a clearer liquid).

3. Decant into a glass bottle and store in the fridge until needed.

4. Shake 100ml of the flavoured vodka with half an egg white (per person) over ice and pour into chilled martini glasses.

Nothing compares to a perfectly roasted chicken; it's a tried and tested staple of everyone's kitchen – you can't mess with that! Chicken is a great choice for feeding friends.

We've put together some simple and versatile dishes for everyone's dinner style; whether you're having a small family gathering, mates round for a party or just an intimate supper for two. Check out our play on 'what came first' with chicken eggs. And it's not just savoury recipes... our eggs and soldiers dessert will definitely get your friends talking!

POP-UP EVENT
HEN PARTY

WHY NOT TRY...
We often like to serve our dishes with an element of surprise. A simple yet delicious plate of Check On nuggets and dips is great for sharing but you could also serve them to your guests individually in personalised little cardboard boxes. It won't cost the earth, will save on washing up and will certainly put a smile on their faces!

Our obsession with chicken began a few years ago. We wanted to create a pop-up event that would really appeal to people who loved chicken as much as we do. So, we dreamt up a Hen Party of chicken themed recipes. We wanted the menu to really excite our guests, offering classics but with our own Check On twist.

GEORGE: I remember before Terry and I even started doing pop-ups together he used to tell me about what he would get up to on quiet lunch services at the Hix Belgravia kitchen in London: how he would be de-boning entire chickens and filling them with more chicken breasts and herb stuffing! Terry was always working on his own 'eggs and soldiers' dessert recipe.

When I tasted it I was blown away. In the prep leading up to these events I was referred to as 'the egg man', as I would be hunched over a sink for about ten hours every Saturday for about three months, cracking and washing egg shells with great care! It was so worth it when you saw people's faces as they opened up the egg boxes to find an amazing dessert.

TERRY: We came up with the name 'Hen Party' and hosted 12 Sunday afternoons in a pub in Soho. People loved our four-course Sunday roast with a great party atmosphere and all-you-can-drink Bloody Marys! We just loved showing people our idea of a good time. George put together a cracking playlist full of playful tunes, from Lionel Richie's 'Dancing on the Ceiling' to Blondie's 'Maria'. Guests were singing along to the songs while eating their meal – it was great fun! It also really brought it home how closely linked food and music are to one another. A memorable meal is not just about the food but the ambience and, of course, great company. That's always been the ethos of Check On.

We were just starting out and although I'd had some experience, it was still a big learning curve in terms of prepping and general organisation for the events. In the early days it was a bit of whirlwind getting everything together, but it was totally worth it. My chicken supplier Reg Johnson used to deliver to London super-early in the morning. He'd pick me up at my flat at about 5 a.m., take me to drop the chickens at the kitchen, then drop me back to my flat for a couple of hours' more sleep. Cheers Reg, a true legend.

20p   50p   £1   £2

You can find a link to this playlist at
checkonpresents.co.uk

GOOD TIMES
CHIC

DANCING ON THE CEILING
LIONEL RICHIE

GET DOWN ON IT
KOOL & THE GANG

SIGNED, SEALED, DELIVERED I'M YOURS
STEVIE WONDER

GET LUCKY
DAFT PUNK

MAGIC CARPET RIDE
STEPPENWOLF

PLAYLIST

MARIA
BLONDIE

SWEET CAROLINE
NEIL DIAMOND

LET'S DANCE
DAVID BOWIE

YOU CAN CALL ME AL
PAUL SIMON

SECOND HAND NEWS
FLEETWOOD MAC

WITH A LITTLE HELP FROM MY FRIENDS
RINGO STARR

CHICKEN AND SWEETCORN CUPPA-SOUP

The key to this and nearly all soups is a good stock. If you haven't time to make your own, we prefer the jelly-style stock cubes to the old chalky powder ones. For some reason, this soup always tastes better in a big mug rather than a bowl but either way it's delicious. It's a meal in itself but could also work well served in smaller cups as a rich first course. A really hearty soup for a cold day that will definitely do the trick if you're under the weather.

SERVES 10–12

4 skinless, boneless
    chicken thighs
50g butter
50g flour
1.5 litres good-quality
    chicken stock (see right)
100ml double cream
150g tinned sweetcorn, drained
1 tbsp finely chopped tarragon

1. Preheat the oven to 180°C/Gas 4.

2. Place the chicken thighs in a roasting tin and roast for 10 minutes until cooked through. Remove from the oven, then flake or chop into chunks.

3. Melt the butter in a heavy-based pan and whisk in the flour to make a roux. Warm your chicken stock in a separate pan.

4. Slowly start to ladle the stock into the roux, whisking continuously to avoid lumps. When all the stock has been incorporated, add the cream, sweetcorn and chopped tarragon and stir together.

5. Place a good spoonful of the flaked chicken into your mug or bowl, then pour over the lovely thick soup.

CHICKEN STOCK

To make your own stock, pop the leftover bones from your roast chicken in a pan, sling in some onions, carrots and celery and cover with cold water. Simmer for 1 hour, topping up the water every now and again, then strain through a sieve and Bob's your uncle.

CHICKEN EGGS

We absolutely love these eggs – they're great eaten hot or cold and are perfect to take on a picnic or for a packed lunch. When we first made these for the Hen Party pop-up event we used quail's eggs... it was an absolute nightmare as they're so hard to peel when soft-boiled. Quail's eggs have been off the menu ever since!

MAKES 6

6 free-range eggs
600g minced chicken breast
   (either mince it yourself or buy
   from your local butcher)
1 tsp thyme leaves
1 tsp finely chopped rosemary
Flour, beaten egg and
   breadcrumbs for coating
Salt and freshly ground
   black pepper
1 litre vegetable oil, for frying
Roasted Garlic Mayo
   (see page 47), to serve

1. Bring a large pan of water to a rolling boil and have a bowl of iced water at the ready. For soft-boiled eggs set a timer for 6 minutes (6½ if your eggs are kept in the fridge).

2. Gently lower the eggs into the pan (we often cook one or two extra in case some don't work out). When the timer goes off, quickly remove the eggs and place in the iced water to stop the cooking process. When the eggs have cooled, carefully peel them and set aside.

3. Place the minced chicken, thyme, rosemary and seasoning in a bowl and mix until well combined. Fry a small amount of the mixture to taste and adjust the seasoning. Divide the chicken mixture into six patties.

4. Roll the peeled eggs in a little flour, then completely wrap each one in a chicken patty, pressing gently with your fingers to seal the join. Chill in the fridge for 20 minutes to firm up the meat, then coat each one in flour, beaten egg and breadcrumbs.

5. Heat the oil in a large, heavy-based pan to 180°C (a cube of bread should sizzle and turn golden immediately). Carefully lower the eggs into the pan, a few at a time, and cook until golden brown, about 8–10 minutes. Remove from the pan with a slotted spoon and drain on kitchen paper while you cook the rest. Season immediately with table salt.

6. Serve immediately or at room temperature with some Roasted Garlic Mayo, or mustard and ketchup.

CHECK ON NUGGETS AND DIPS

TERRY: I loved the takeaway version of chicken nuggets when I was young and a big basket of these chicken dippers will put a smile on anyone's face. Something about the buttermilk batter makes all the difference – you'll never go back!

SERVES 4

6 chicken breast fillets,
    cut into 3cm pieces
300ml buttermilk
Zest and juice of 1 lemon
300g rice crispies
2 tsp chilli powder
1 tsp ground cumin
1 tbsp flour
2 tsp paprika
1 tsp dried oregano
1 tsp mustard powder
1 tsp pepper
2 tsp salt

1. Place the diced chicken in a large bowl with the buttermilk, zest and lemon juice and leave to marinate for a couple of hours.

2. Preheat the oven to 180°C/Gas 4.

3. Mix all the remaining ingredients together, lightly crushing the rice crispies. Remove the chicken pieces from the buttermilk one at a time and toss in the seasoning mix, then place on a non-stick baking tray.

4. Place the chicken in the oven and cook for 5 minutes before turning and cooking for another 4 minutes until crispy and cooked through.

FLAVOURED MAYO

Mayo is such a versatile condiment – smooth and creamy with just the right amount of tang from the vinegar, it's absolutely lovely on its own. But it really shines when it's combined with other ingredients as a base to another sauce or dressing. Here are a few of my favourite ways to use it!

STRAIGHT-UP MAYO

4 large free-range egg yolks
2 tsp English mustard
Splash of white wine vinegar
600ml vegetable oil
Sea salt and white pepper

Place the egg yolks, mustard, the white wine vinegar and a pinch of sea salt and white pepper in a food processor or blender and blitz to combine. Slowly trickle in the vegetable oil in a very thin stream. Take care not to split the mayo – patience is key! If the mayo does start to split, a little warm water can sometimes do the job to bring it back. You can also thin the mayo with a little warm water if it is too thick.

CAESAR MAYO DRESSING

6 salted anchovy fillets
  (with a little oil from the tin)
1 garlic clove
1 tbsp grated Parmesan
5 tbsp mayonnaise
1 tbsp warm water
Freshly ground black pepper

Use a pestle and mortar to grind
together the anchovy fillets, a
drizzle of oil from the tin, the
garlic and Parmesan. Add the
anchovy paste to the mayo and
mix well, adding the warm water to
loosen the mixture a little. Season
to taste with black pepper.

TARRAGON MAYO

5 tbsp mayonnaise
2 tsp finely chopped tarragon
Squeeze of lemon juice

Combine all the ingredients
together in a bowl and mix
thoroughly.

ROASTED GARLIC MAYO

10 garlic cloves
Rapeseed oil
5 tbsp mayonnaise
Sea salt and freshly ground
  black pepper

Preheat the oven to 160°C/Gas 3.
Place the garlic cloves in a shallow
roasting tin, drizzle generously
with rapeseed oil
and season with salt and pepper.
Roast for 20 minutes, until the
garlic is soft and lightly golden.
Allow to cool, then tip the garlic
and any oil from the roasting tin
into a food processor or blender
and blitz to a smooth paste. Stir
into the mayonnaise.

MUSTARD MAYO

5 tbsp mayonnaise
2 tsp English mustard
2 tsp wholegrain mustard

Combine all the ingredients
together in a bowl and mix
thoroughly.

SMOKY KETCHUP

*This is a nice way to kick your
ketchup up a notch when you want
a bit of extra spice.*

200g tomato ketchup
1 tsp smoked paprika
½ tsp cayenne pepper
Good glug of
  Worcestershire sauce

Combine all the ingredients
together in a bowl and mix
thoroughly.

CHICKEN AND GIROLLE PIE

Girolles have a light, delicate flavour. They're utterly delicious and take the humble chicken and mushroom pie to the next level. This dish was inspired by a big staff meal we rustled up after one of our Hen Party pop-ups. We had a kilo of girolles and about 15 chicken breasts left over. We popped to the shop to get some ready-rolled puff pastry and the rest is history! You can cook this in one large family-style dish (about 22cm in diameter) or in individual pie dishes.

SERVES 4–6

500g girolle mushrooms
2 tbsp rapeseed oil
4 skinless chicken breasts,
    cut into 3cm pieces
1 onion, diced
2 garlic cloves, finely chopped
60g unsalted butter
2 tbsp plain flour
200ml whole milk
200ml chicken stock
100ml double cream
1 tbsp freshly chopped parsley
1 tbsp freshly chopped tarragon
330g ready-rolled puff pastry
2 egg yolks, lightly beaten
Salt and freshly ground
    black pepper

1. Preheat the oven to 180°C/Gas 4.

2. First (and most importantly) wash your mushrooms in a clean sink filled with cold water to remove any traces of grit. Repeat this process three times, then pat the mushrooms dry on kitchen paper.

3. Heat the oil in a large, heavy-based pan over a medium heat and fry the chicken pieces until just starting to colour, then add the onion and garlic and fry until softened.

4. Add the mushrooms and increase the heat to high to evaporate the water from them until the pan is almost dry again.

5. Melt the butter in a separate pan over a medium heat, add the flour, stirring well, and cook for a minute or two to make a roux. Mix together the milk, stock and cream and slowly add to the roux, whisking all the time, until you have a smooth creamy sauce. Stir in the parsley and tarragon and remove from the heat.

6. Unroll the pastry sheet on a floured board. Turn the pie tin or casserole dish you are using upside down on to the pastry and use a sharp knife to cut out the shape of the lid (or lids if you are making individual pies).

7. Add the chicken and mushroom mixture to the sauce and combine gently, then tip into your pie dish or dishes and allow to cool before topping with the pastry. Press the edges gently to seal, then use a pastry brush to brush the egg yolks over the pastry. Pierce a hole in the top of the pie to let some steam out when cooking.

8. Bake for 25–30 minutes, or until the top is crisp and golden. Bring the piping-hot pie to the table and let everyone dig in. We like to serve this with some roasted vegetables or a fresh salad of dressed green beans.

ROAST CHICKEN WITH TARRAGON AND LEMON BUTTER

A classic favourite. The tarragon and lemon butter is lovely and fresh combined with the roasting juices. Whenever we make this, it never gets to the table in one piece – or at least with the skin intact! The butter is so versatile – try it stirred through pasta with some flaked chicken leg meat.

SERVES 4

2 carrots, roughly chopped
1 celery stick, roughly chopped
2 onions, roughly chopped
1 whole garlic bulb,
    cut in half horizontally
1.8kg free-range chicken
Salt and freshly ground
    black pepper

For the tarragon and lemon butter –
150g softened butter
Small bunch of fresh tarragon,
    woody stalks removed
Zest and juice of 1 lemon

1. Preheat the oven to 200°C/Gas 6.

2. Arrange the carrot, celery, onions and garlic in a single layer in the bottom of an ovenproof dish and place the chicken on top. Make slits in the legs and thighs (this will help the leg meat cook at the same time as the breast meat) and season generously with salt and pepper. Add a splash of water (to catch the roasting juices and prevent them from evaporating).

3. Place the butter, tarragon, lemon zest and juice and a pinch of pepper in a food processor. Blitz on high speed until all the ingredients are combined. Rub the butter on to the legs and push some under the skin.

4. Place in the oven and roast for 50 minutes to 1 hour. When the skin is nice and crispy and the juices run clear when the thickest part of the chicken is pierced with a knife, remove from the oven and leave to rest for 20 minutes.

5. Serve on a platter with the roasting juices and sweet sticky veg. See the 'Sunday Dinners' section for how to make the perfect roast potatoes.

LEMON PAVLOVA WITH MERRY BERRIES

Pavlova is a showstopper of a dessert, plus it's great for feeding a crowd and can be made in advance, which cuts down on stress. This version not only tastes fantastic but looks stunning too. The sweet sugary lemon meringue is perfectly complemented by the tartness of the berries and the silky smooth whipped cream. We make the berries 'merry' by adding cassis to the jam. Crack open some lovely chilled sparkling wine and enjoy.

SERVES 6–8

4 egg whites
250g caster sugar
1 tsp cornflour
1 tsp white wine vinegar
Zest of 2 lemons
250ml double cream
1 vanilla pod, slit lengthways
    and seeds scraped out
50ml crème de cassis, plus extra
    for drizzling
100g blackberry jam
200g blackberries
100g blueberries
Handful of baby mint leaves
Icing sugar, for dusting

1. Preheat the oven to 130°C/ Gas ½ and line a baking tray with parchment paper.

2. Whisk the egg whites in a very clean bowl until they form stiff peaks, then gradually whisk in the sugar, cornflour, white wine vinegar and lemon zest.

3. Spread the meringue on to the lined baking tray, roughly 8cm high, either in a rough circle or rectangle shape (depending on what dish you want to serve it on). Bake in the oven for 55 minutes, then turn off the oven and leave the meringue inside for a few hours to cool. This is a great tip to stop the meringue cracking.

4. When you are ready to serve, whip the cream and vanilla seeds together until stiff peaks form and set aside.

5. Mix together the cassis and blackberry jam and spread over the pavlova. Scatter the berries and mint leaves over the top and drizzle with some extra cassis. Top with the vanilla cream and a sprinkle of icing sugar.

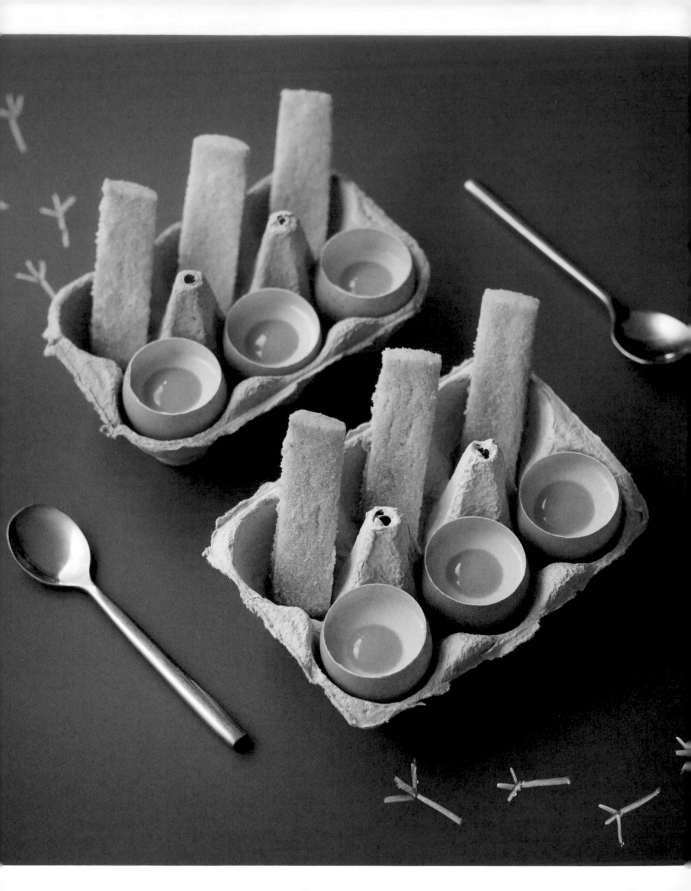

EGGS AND SOLDIERS

This is actually a quite simple yet delicious dessert of set vanilla cream with a thick mango purée, but it's all about the presentation here, which will take you back to being a kid again. EVERYONE takes a picture of this one! It has become our signature dish and we still love making it. We serve this in hollowed-out eggshells. If you'd like to do the same, you'll need an egg topper, available from any good catering shop or online. Alternatively you can use ramekins. These are great if you're throwing a party. Put a big box on the table and watch them go! If you're having a sit-down dinner you can serve them in a six-egg box (see opposite).

SERVES 6–8

For the vanilla cream
600ml double cream
1 vanilla pod
8 egg yolks
50g caster sugar

For the mango jelly
2 sheets of leaf gelatine
150ml mango purée (either shop-bought purée or mango smoothie)
40g caster sugar

For the shortbread fingers
100g caster sugar, plus extra for sprinkling
200g butter, softened
300g plain flour, plus extra for dusting

1. Pour the cream into a small, heavy-based pan and slit the vanilla pod in half lengthways. Scrape out the seeds and put the pod and seeds into the pan with the cream. Bring just to the boil over a low-medium heat.

2. Meanwhile put the egg yolks and caster sugar into a medium-sized heatproof bowl and stir until just combined. As soon as the cream comes to the boil, remove the vanilla pods and pour the cream on to the yolk and sugar mixture, stirring continuously.

3. Return the egg and cream mixture to the pan and gently cook over a low heat until the mixture thickens up (it should coat the back of a spoon). Pour the mixture into the eggshells or ramekins and place in the fridge for 1 hour.

4. For the mango jelly, soften the gelatine for a few minutes in a bowl of cold water. Meanwhile, gently warm the mango purée in a small pan, add the caster sugar and stir until it has dissolved. Once the gelatine has softened, remove from the water and squeeze out the excess water. Add it to the warm mango mixture and stir thoroughly, then set aside to cool and set.

5. Meanwhile make the shortbread. Cream together the sugar and butter until well combined, then stir in the flour. Use your hands to bring it all together and work until you have a smooth dough. Wrap in cling film and chill in the fridge for 30 minutes while you preheat the oven to 160°C/Gas 3.

6. Remove the dough from the fridge and roll out on a lightly floured surface to a thickness of about 1cm. Cut into 8–10 fingers, place on a baking tray and bake in the oven for about 20 minutes, or until lightly coloured. Sprinkle with a little caster sugar while they are still warm and leave to cool (this is the hardest part!).

7. Place a teaspoon of the cold mango jelly on to each of the cream-filled eggs or ramekins and serve with shortbread fingers.

BLOODY MARY WITH SMOKY KETCHUP

For us, a Bloody Mary is the perfect hangover cure (that and a bacon sandwich, obviously). A good one is all about the seasoning. Serve this if you're making a late Sunday lunch and you know your guests have had a big Saturday night!

GEORGE: I like mine quite salty.

TERRY: I prefer mine with a good hit of Tabasco. This is definitely a 'season to taste' kind of drink.

SERVES 4–5

Pint glass of ice, plus extra
   to serve
250ml good-quality vodka
Juice of 2 lemons
2 tsp Worcestershire sauce
1 tsp Tabasco sauce
500ml tomato juice
100ml Smoky Ketchup
   (see page 47)
Sea salt and freshly ground
   black pepper
4–5 celery sticks, peeled

1. Place the ice in a large jug and add all the ingredients except the celery. Stir well, then taste and adjust the seasoning, adding more of whatever you think it needs.

2. Fill 4 or 5 tall (highball) glasses with ice and distribute the Bloody Mary evenly between them. Pop a celery stick in each one and drink immediately.

VENISON BURGER

VEAL MEATBALLS WITH GARLIC AND CHILLI

HASH STAG #

KING BEEF WELLINGTON

ROASTED DUCK BREAST WITH PICKLED PEACHES AND CELERIAC

MASH FIVE WAYS

ROASTED JERUSALEM ARTICHOKES WITH LEMON AND TARRAGON MAYONNAISE

BRAISED CELERY HEARTS WITH PARSLEY AND LEMON

POACHED PEARS WITH LEMON THYME MASCARPONE CREAM

OLD FASHIONED WITH ORANGE ICE CUBES

This chapter is our unadulterated meat-fest, a guide to cooking some great gamey meats like venison and duck (as well as beef) and the perfect accompaniments to go with them. Pop into your local butcher and ask him for some minced venison and we're pretty sure the next time you go in, he'll remember your name. While a quality cut of meat can be expensive, the flavour and richness of the meat means it can go a long way in terms of how many you can feed! Prod, poke and feel your steaks and burgers while they're cooking. The general rule is that the springier your meat, the more it's cooked. So, super bouncy is going to be well done, nice and soft is going to be rare and in between is, well... medium.

The recipes here are all about making meat the star of the show, whether you're making burgers for friends, a casual Friday night supper of meatballs or the venison 'hash stag' as a romantic meal for two.

POP-UP EVENT
STAG PARTY

WHY NOT TRY...

We always love a cheeky cocktail at the start of the night – and at the end too! We'll often have a bottle of vodka infused with fruit in the fridge, which we'll pull out at the end of a meal to lift everyone out of a food coma! Another alternative is freezing berries or even cordials such as elderflower in ice-cube trays, which you can quickly turn out into a glass of gin. It's a great way to round off a lovely evening with friends.

TERRY: We followed up our 'Hen Party' pop-up the only way we knew how: with a 'Stag Party'. We wanted to celebrate meat in all its glory and put together a menu based around venison – dishes such as venison with cherries, a burger with game chips and, to round off the meal, whiskey jellies. The Hen Party tickets were cheap, considering you got a four-course meal with a Bloody Mary thrown in for good measure, and I remember thinking, 'Oh god, what if nobody wants to come because we've had to put the prices up to cover the cost of the venison?' But they did. I think people were interested as we were doing something different. The food was still playful but a bit refined too.

GEORGE: I remember travelling all around London on the day leading up to the event, picking up various cuts of venison from guys in the back entrances of butchers and kitchens. It was quite an adventure and I remember receiving bemused looks when I rocked up in my chrome Burberry trenchcoat fresh off a photo shoot. For me it was a real moment of my different lives colliding! Then it was back to the kitchen where a mountain of potatoes awaited me, ready for peeling and prepping for the game chips we had on the menu. We had a lot of fun putting the playlist together for the event, paying homage to some of the greatest 70s soul icons, such as Curtis Mayfield and James Brown. For us, Stag Party was about drawing on achingly cool old school glamour with a bit of *The Godfather* thrown in for good measure!

20p 50p £1 £2

You can find a link to this playlist at
checkonpresents.co.uk

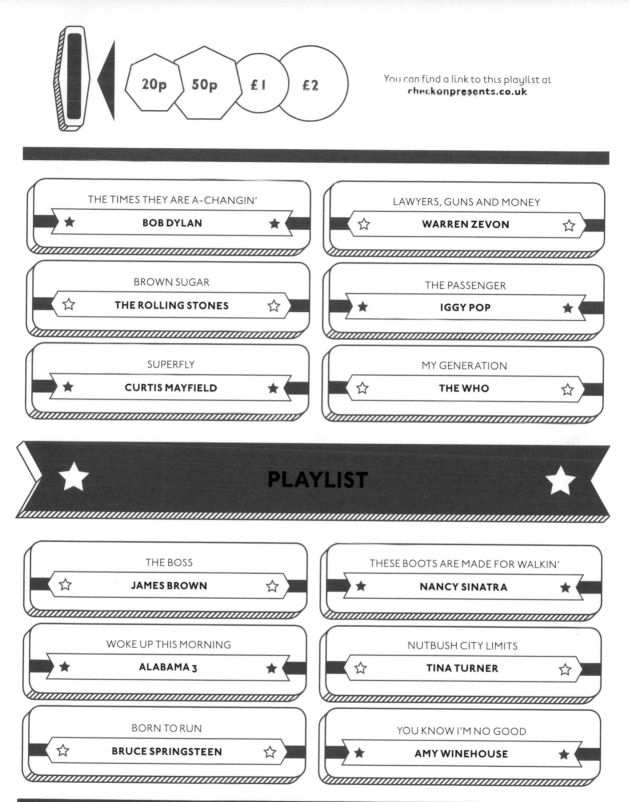

THE TIMES THEY ARE A-CHANGIN'
BOB DYLAN

LAWYERS, GUNS AND MONEY
WARREN ZEVON

BROWN SUGAR
THE ROLLING STONES

THE PASSENGER
IGGY POP

SUPERFLY
CURTIS MAYFIELD

MY GENERATION
THE WHO

PLAYLIST

THE BOSS
JAMES BROWN

THESE BOOTS ARE MADE FOR WALKIN'
NANCY SINATRA

WOKE UP THIS MORNING
ALABAMA 3

NUTBUSH CITY LIMITS
TINA TURNER

BORN TO RUN
BRUCE SPRINGSTEEN

YOU KNOW I'M NO GOOD
AMY WINEHOUSE

VENISON BURGER

If you've never had venison before, a burger is the greatest way to be introduced to this lovely, lean, rich, flavoursome meat. Venison lends itself really well to being cooked medium-rare and that's how we cook it here. Remember... prod, poke and feel! It goes great with some really salty crispy bacon and some tangy pickled cucumber.

SERVES 5

For the burger
25g butter
½ tsp ground cumin
1 large onion, finely diced
1 garlic clove, crushed
800g coarsely minced venison
1 egg, beaten
100g chopped fresh coriander
100g chopped fresh parsley
Salt and freshly ground
    black pepper
Olive oil, for frying

To serve
5 brioche buns, lightly toasted
10 slices of crispy smoked bacon
5 thin slices of beef tomato
Pickled Cucumber (see page 101)

1. Melt the butter in a pan over a low-medium heat and gently fry the cumin with the onion and garlic for about 5 minutes until softened, then set aside to cool. Once cooled, tip into a bowl with the remaining ingredients, except the olive oil, and mix thoroughly to combine.

2. Whenever you're making a batch of something like this, it's always a good idea to fry a small amount to check for seasoning. Roll a small amount into a ball, fry and then adjust the seasoning as necessary.

3. Divide the burger mix into 5 fist-sized balls and form into patties. Season with salt and pepper and rub with a little olive oil. Place a large frying pan over a medium-high heat until smoking hot and add the patties. Cook for 3–5 minutes on each side, turning carefully.

4. Assemble the burgers in the lightly toasted brioche buns with layers of crispy bacon, beef tomato and pickled cucumber.

VEAL MEATBALLS WITH GARLIC AND CHILLI

This is the ultimate sharing dish. It's all about dropping a massive plate of it in the middle of a table and letting everyone just crack on. We love watching old mafia films, where the food is such a big part of the family tradition. They all argue who has the best tomato sauce or meatballs... forget about it! These are just as delicious if you replace the veal with beef.

SERVES 4–6

For the meatballs
700g veal or beef mince
2 garlic cloves, crushed
100g grated Parmesan
200g granary breadcrumbs
2 eggs, beaten
1 tsp lemon thyme leaves
1 tbsp vegetable oil

For the sauce
1–2 tbsp olive oil
1 large onion, finely chopped
5 garlic cloves, finely chopped
3 celery sticks, finely chopped
2 carrots, finely chopped
2 large red chillies, roughly
   chopped (leave the seeds in)
½ tsp thyme leaves
250ml red wine
1kg chopped tinned tomatoes
1 bunch of basil, stalks removed
   and leaves torn
Salt and freshly ground
   black pepper

1. To make the meatballs, combine all the ingredients except the oil in a large bowl and mix together thoroughly. Fry a small amount of the mixture in a pan to test for seasoning, then roll the rest into balls, about 50–60g each (you should get 15–20 meatballs from this amount). Chill in the fridge for 20–30 minutes before frying.

2. Meanwhile make the sauce. Heat the oil in a large heavy-based pan over a medium heat. Add the onion, garlic, celery, carrots, chillies and thyme leaves and cook gently until the onions are translucent and the vegetables are soft.

3. Increase the heat and add the red wine; let it bubble until reduced by half. Add the chopped tomatoes, bring to a gentle boil, then reduce the heat and leave to simmer for 30 minutes.

4. Heat the oil in a large frying pan and fry the meatballs, in small batches, until browned on all sides. Add to the sauce and allow to simmer for a further 10–15 minutes, until the meatballs are cooked through.

5. Add the basil leaves and serve with some cooked pasta... go classic with spaghetti or, if you're wearing a white shirt, go for the safer option of penne or rigatoni.

HASH STAG

We were sitting in George's living room in Yorkshire talking about recipe names and our friend Simon came up with 'Hash Stag'. We were sold and ran with it and that's how this dish was born. Venison is quite an expensive meat but a real treat for a special occasion dinner or a romantic meal for two. Its rich, almost oaky flavour needs the sharp twang of a fruity sauce to balance it out and that's what the blackberries in this recipe do perfectly. If you can forage for some berries that will save you a few quid... every little helps!

SERVES 2

2 x 200g venison fillets
1 tbsp olive oil

For the blackberry sauce
20g butter
1 banana shallot, finely chopped
300g fresh blackberries
3 tsp redcurrant jelly
½ tsp chopped fresh
    thyme leaves
100ml dark chicken stock

For the hash
1 large potato, grated
1 red onion, finely sliced
2 spring onions, finely sliced
1 sprig of rosemary,
    leaves finely chopped
40g butter
Salt and freshly ground
    black pepper

1. First make the sauce. Melt the butter in a pan over a low-medium heat and soften the shallots until translucent. Add the blackberries, redcurrant jelly, thyme and stock. Bring to the boil and cook to reduce the liquid by half, then pass through a fine sieve into a bowl. Remove the blackberries from the sieve and return them to the strained liquid. Set aside until ready to serve.

2. Combine the potato, red onion, spring onions and rosemary for the hash in a bowl and season with salt and pepper. Leave for 5 minutes; this will draw some moisture out of the potatoes and onions, helping to achieve a crispy texture.

3. Transfer the potato and onion mix to a clean bowl, squeezing the excess liquid from the mixture with your hands as you go.

4. Heat the butter in a frying pan over a medium heat, then add the squeezed potato mix, pressing down to spread out and compact it.

Cook for 5 minutes, then carefully lift up the hash with a spatula and check that the underside is golden brown. Carefully flip over and cook for a further 5 minutes on the other side.

5. Meanwhile cook the venison fillets. Place a frying pan over a medium-high heat until smoking hot. Season the venison generously with salt and pepper. Add the olive oil to the pan, followed by the venison fillets. Cook for 4–5 minutes on each side for medium rare, 6–7 for medium. Remove the fillets from the pan and leave to rest for 3 minutes before serving.

6. To serve, slice the rested venison and place on top of the hash. Season the meat with a sprinkle of sea salt and spoon over the blackberry sauce.

KING BEEF WELLINGTON

GEORGE: One Friday we were finishing a pop-up and I was heading out of town to the studio so Terry gave me some beef mince, beef fillet and rib-eye steaks to take with me. When they saw the amount of beef I'd brought with me the guys decided to call me 'King Beef' for the week. I phoned Terry and asked what I should make with the beef fillet and here's what we came up with. A far cry from the old days on tour surviving on service station and takeaway food.

SERVES 6–8

800g beef fillet
½ tbsp olive oil
250g button mushrooms,
    very finely chopped
50ml double cream
English mustard, for brushing
2 tsp fresh thyme leaves
500g shop-bought puff pastry
3 egg yolks, beaten
Sea salt and freshly ground
    black pepper

For the pancakes

110g plain flour
2 eggs
200ml milk
Salt and freshly ground
    black pepper
Butter, for frying

1. First make the pancakes. Whisk the flour, eggs and milk together in a bowl until smooth and free of lumps. Season with salt and pepper. Lightly grease a large frying pan with butter and pour in a ladle or two of the batter to make a nice, thin pancake. Turn and cook the other side, remove from the pan and repeat with the remaining batter to make four pancakes. Set aside to cool.

2. Season the beef fillet and rub all over with a little olive oil, then sear in a hot, dry frying pan until browned on all sides. Remove from the pan and set aside to cool.

3. Add the chopped mushrooms to the same pan and fry them over a medium heat for 10 minutes, seasoning generously with salt and pepper. Cook until all the excess water has evaporated, then add the cream and reduce by half. Set aside to cool.

4. When the beef fillet has cooled completely, brush generously all over with English mustard, season with salt and pepper and sprinkle with the thyme leaves.

5. Arrange the pancakes on your work surface so that they overlap each other and spread over the cooled mushroom mixture. Place the fillet in the middle and fold the pancakes over the top to completely encase the beef, trimming away any excess pancake. Roll the pancake-wrapped fillet tightly in cling film and chill in the fridge for 1 hour.

6. Preheat the oven to 180°C/ Gas 4 while you roll out the puff pastry on a lightly floured surface. Take the chilled fillet from the fridge, remove the cling film and repeat the wrapping process with the puff pastry, sealing the edges with beaten egg yolk. Place seam side down on a baking tray and brush all over with the egg yolk to glaze. Sprinkle with a little sea salt and cook in the oven until done to your liking: 30 minutes for rare, 35 minutes for medium and 40 minutes for well done.

ROASTED DUCK BREAST WITH PICKLED PEACHES AND CELERIAC

TERRY: I love this because for me it's such a seasonal crossover dish. In the summer when peaches are at their best, we use them fresh torn into salads, grilled with ice cream or thinly sliced with some lovely salty cured ham. But as we come to the end of the summer we start to pop them into pickling liquor and will forget about them for 4–5 weeks. Before we know it it's autumn, and we can use them with some earthy celeriac and pink corn-fed duck breast. It's a lovely reminder of the summer, just as you start to feel winter creeping in.

SERVES 5

1 large celeriac, peeled and
    cut into chunks
4 garlic cloves
400ml full-fat milk
150ml cream
100g butter
5 corn-fed duck breasts, skin on
10 Pickled Peach halves
    (see page 100)
Salt and freshly ground
    black pepper

1. Preheat the oven to 180°C/Gas 4.

2. First prepare the celeriac. Place the celeriac chunks and garlic cloves in a heavy-based pan with the milk, cream and butter. Season with salt and pepper and bring to the boil. Reduce the heat and simmer until the celeriac is tender, about 15–20 minutes. Transfer the celeriac, garlic and cooking liquid to a blender and pulse until you have a rough purée. Taste and adjust the seasoning, then return to the pan and set aside until ready to serve.

3. Gently score the skin on the duck breasts with a sharp knife; this will help release the fat when cooking. Season the duck breasts with salt and pepper and place skin side down in a large, cold, ovenproof frying pan.

Cook over a low-medium heat for 10 minutes. Drain away the fat from the pan before placing in the oven for a further 5 minutes for medium-rare. Remove from the oven and allow to rest for 3–5 minutes before slicing.

4. Gently warm the peaches in the oven while the duck is resting.

5. To serve, reheat the celeriac and. arrange on plates. Top with the duck slices and peach halves.

MASH FIVE WAYS

The first thing to mention is that you need to buy a potato ricer and get rid of your old-school potato masher; it's key to getting that smooth, lump-free mashed potato. We use Maris Piper potatoes for our mash, but any floury potato will do.

ALL RECIPES SERVE 3–4 PEOPLE

GARLIC MASH

600g Maris Piper potatoes,
    peeled and cut into chunks
10 garlic cloves
100ml double cream
150g cold butter, diced
Salt and freshly ground
    black pepper

1. Place the potatoes and garlic in a large pan of salted water and bring to the boil. Cook for about 15–20 minutes, or until the potatoes are tender when pierced with a knife.

2. Drain the potatoes and garlic and squeeze them both through a potato ricer back into the pan. Place the pan over a medium heat and gradually add the cream. Beat in the butter until smooth and season with salt and pepper.

ENGLISH MUSTARD MASH

600g Maris Piper potatoes,
    peeled and cut into chunks
100ml double cream
150g cold butter, diced
50g English mustard, or to taste
Salt and freshly ground
    black pepper

1. Place the potatoes in a large pan of salted water and bring to the boil. Cook for about 15–20 minutes, or until the potatoes are tender when pierced with a knife.

2. Drain the potatoes and squeeze them through a potato ricer back into the pan. Place the pan over a medium heat and gradually add the cream. Beat in the butter until smooth and season with salt and pepper.

3. Add the mustard, mix thoroughly and check the seasoning. I like to add 50g of English mustard but it's very much a case of adding as much or as little as you like.

COLCANNON

600g Maris Piper potatoes,
    peeled and cut into chunks
75ml double cream
100ml full-fat milk
200g Savoy cabbage, thinly sliced
150g cold butter, diced
Salt and freshly ground
    black pepper

1. Place the potatoes in a large pan of salted water and bring to the boil. Cook for about 15–20 minutes, or until the potatoes are tender when pierced with a knife.

2. Drain the potatoes and squeeze them through a potato ricer back into the pan.

3. In a separate pan, bring the cream and milk to the boil and add the finely sliced cabbage. Cook for a couple of minutes until the cabbage is tender.

4. Place the pan of potatoes over a medium heat and gradually beat in the butter until smooth, then pour the cream, milk and cabbage into the potatoes and mix thoroughly. Season with salt and pepper (I like to give this a really good hit of black pepper to spice it up).

RED ONION MASH

600g Maris Piper potatoes,
  peeled and cut into chunks
150g cold butter, diced
2 red onions, thinly sliced
100ml double cream
Salt and freshly ground
  black pepper

1. Place the potatoes in a large pan of salted water and bring to the boil. Cook for about 15–20 minutes, or until the potatoes are tender when pierced with a knife.

2. Meanwhile, melt 50g of the butter in a frying pan and gently fry the red onions over a low-medium heat until softened, about 10 minutes.

3. Drain the potatoes and squeeze them through a potato ricer back into the pan. Place the pan over a medium heat and gradually add the cream. Beat in the remaining butter until smooth. Stir in the softened onions and season generously with salt and pepper.

CHEDDAR MASH

600g Maris Piper potatoes,
  peeled and cut into chunks
150ml crème fraîche
100g cold butter, diced
200g grated Cheddar
Salt and freshly ground
  black pepper

1. Preheat the oven to 180°C/Gas 4.

2. Place the potatoes in a large pan of salted water and bring to the boil. Cook for about 15–20 minutes, or until the potatoes are tender when pierced with a knife.

3. Drain the potatoes and squeeze them through a potato ricer back into the pan. Add the crème fraîche and the butter and beat until smooth.

4. Pile the mash into an ovenproof dish, top with the grated Cheddar and place in the oven for 10 minutes, until the cheese is melted and bubbling.

ROASTED JERUSALEM ARTICHOKES WITH LEMON AND TARRAGON MAYONNAISE

For years I used to peel these beautiful, knobbly things and discard the skin. Now I love them just washed and roasted in their skin – it has so much flavour! These are a great alternative to roast potatoes.

SERVES 4–6

800g Jerusalem artichokes,
    washed
2 tbsp rapeseed oil or duck fat
Zest of 1 lemon
Salt and freshly ground
    black pepper
Tarragon Mayonnaise
    (see page 47)

1. Preheat the oven to 180°C/Gas 4.

2. Cut the artichokes into bite-sized pieces and arrange in a single layer on a baking tray. Drizzle with the oil and season generously with salt and pepper. Roast in the oven for 25–30 minutes, or until tender in the middle when pierced with a knife.

3. Tip the roasted artichokes on to a serving plate and grate over the lemon zest. Serve with some Tarragon Mayonnaise on the side.

BRAISED CELERY HEARTS WITH PARSLEY AND LEMON

Celery is usually finely chopped and fried with onions and carrots as a base for soup or for stocks and sauces. There's nothing wrong with that, of course, but this dish gives celery the starring role. It's a great accompaniment to red meat and chicken.

SERVES 4

3 whole celery hearts,
 cut lengthways and leafy
 tops trimmed
2 tbsp rapeseed oil
1 small onion, thinly sliced
3 garlic cloves, finely chopped
100ml white wine
300ml light chicken stock
Juice of 1 lemon
1 tbsp finely chopped parsley
Salt and freshly ground
 black pepper

1. Preheat the oven to 180°C/Gas 4.

2. Bring a large pan of salted water to a rolling boil and part-cook the celery for 5 minutes. Remove from the pan and drain on kitchen paper.

3. Heat the oil in a heavy-based roasting tin (or use a high-sided ovenproof frying pan) and add the celery hearts, cut side down. Fry over a medium heat until golden brown on one side.

4. Add the onion and garlic to the pan and soften for a few minutes before adding the wine. Let it bubble and reduce by half. Add the chicken stock and place in the oven for about 20 minutes, until the celery is tender.

5. Transfer to a dish and pour over the lovely roasting juices. Squeeze over the lemon juice and scatter with the parsley before serving.

POACHED PEARS WITH LEMON THYME MASCARPONE CREAM

TERRY: We used to have a pear tree in our back yard when I was a kid, which is basically how this dish came about. I'm not going to wistfully tell you that they were great because they were, in fact, hard, flavourless and bloody awful. But, undeterred, the experience encouraged me to always try pear desserts on menus. Eating poached pears in Italy inspired me to create this dish. This is a fairly light pudding, ideal for serving if you've had a big meaty main. You can also make this in advance.

SERVES 4

4 Williams pears, peeled
   but stalks left on

For the poaching liquor ————
500g caster sugar
500ml red wine
200ml water
I star anise
I cinnamon stick
2 sprigs of thyme
I clove

For the cream ————
150g mascarpone
60ml double cream
Zest of 2 lemons
1/2 tsp lemon thyme leaves

1. Put all the ingredients for the poaching liquor in a heavy-based pan and bring to the boil. Add the pears and reduce the heat to a simmer.

2. Check the pears after 15 minutes with a knife to see if it slides in easily. If they are still hard, continue to cook and check again after a few minutes. Remove from the heat and allow to cool.

3. Remove the pears from the pan and strain the poaching liquor through a fine sieve into a clean pan. Place back on the heat and reduce to a syrupy consistency; set aside.

4. Place all the ingredients for the cream in a large bowl and mix well.

5. Halve the pears and arrange on a large plate, drizzle over the reduced poaching liquid and serve with dollops of the cream.

OLD FASHIONED WITH ORANGE ICE CUBES

It's great to bring out a tray of these after dinner with friends. The orange ice cubes add a touch of citrus to the oaky smoky bourbon.

SERVES 4

Peel and juice of 1 orange
200ml water
4 brown sugar cubes
4 dashes of orange angostura
    bitters
200ml good bourbon whiskey
1 blood orange, sliced, to garnish
    (optional)

1. First make the orange ice cubes – at least 4 hours before you want to serve the drink. Use a potato peeler to pare the orange peel into strips, then squeeze the juice into a bowl, removing any stray pips that fall into the liquid. Stir in the water and divide into a large ice-cube tray. Gently push a piece of orange peel into each compartment and place the tray in the freezer.

2. Take 4 tumblers (old fashioned glasses) and add a sugar cube and a dash of angostura bitters to each one. Crush the sugar cube until dissolved with a muddler (if you don't have one of these bar tools you can use a pestle or the back of a wooden spoon).

3. Add 50ml of the bourbon and a few ice cubes to each glass; stir each drink for 30 seconds to allow the ice to dissolve a little and dilute the drink. Garnish with a slice of blood orange, if using, and serve immediately.

CHICKEN DONER KEBAB —————————————————

LAMB KEBAB WITH POMEGRANATE ————————————

CHECK ON CHILLI SAUCE ——————————————————

FISH FINGERS AND CURRY SAUCE ————————————

THE ULTIMATE STEAK SANDWICH ——————————————

JALAPEÑO MAC AND CHEESE ——————————————————

PICKLES ————————————————————————————

BURNT SALTED CARAMEL ICE CREAM ——————————

CHOCOLATE RICE PUDDING WITH TOASTED MARSHMALLOWS ———

BRAMBLE SNAKEBITE —————————————————

We are a nation of take-out and junk food eaters. We're not saying that's what we eat every day and night, but let's face it: we all love a good kebab after a night out every now and again. This chapter means that you no longer have to keep this hidden, with our tasty versions of fish fingers and curry sauce, lamb doner kebabs and jalapeño mac and cheese – food packed full of flavour and made for sharing.

The dishes in this section are absolutely perfect party food – whether you're throwing a birthday bash for a friend, or as a great alternative to having people over on a warm, summer evening, where you don't fancy doing a barbecue but want to serve up plenty of buffet-style food.

POP-UP EVENT
KEBAB FINGERS

WHY NOT TRY...

If you are going for more of a lively, party atmosphere think about the things that will create the right vibe, such as how you can light the room: we're a big fan of fairy lights and candles… and, given that we're talking guilty pleasures here, why not go all out with a disco ball? You could also have a bottle of tequila on ice on display, which instantly sets the tone of the evening to come…

GEORGE: I had never eaten a kebab in my life until about 2013… All those years on tour round the UK and I'd been missing out on this guilty pleasure. I'd see the rest of my band wrapping their faces around a mixed meat doner after a night out celebrating an amazing show and always pass on it. To be honest I was just more than happy with a good bag of salt and vinegar discos. Terry introduced me to the absolute sin that is the doner kebab. (He hasn't only introduced my palate to naughty food – I had my first oysters with him too.)

We wanted to try our hand at making some doner kebabs and had the idea of doing a short residency of Check On style takeaway food, so we started to look into possible venues. While we were looking we invited our neighbours round (we knew they occasionally had a few pints down the pub followed by a kebab). They were really excited by our take on the humble kebab and we thought 'we're onto a winner here!'

TERRY: We ordered in Yorkshire's finest minced lamb from the Ginger Pig farm and got to work. Some of the kebabs on offer included a cumin-spiced lamb doner with roasted peppers, pickled shallots and mint yoghurt, a pomegranate-glazed chicken kebab with roasted garlic, lemon mayo and sultanas and a grilled halloumi, oven-dried tomato and roasted chilli kebab. It was a really fun night and we set up the food in a way that everybody just built their own meals. We had the BEST time putting the playlist together for this event. It was a real 'no holding back' moment. I added some of my favourite classic Phil Collins tracks (and yes I am a huge fan of his!) and George dug out his beloved Abba records. It was a great way of bringing people together. I remember seeing everyone smiling, letting their hair down and having a bit of a dance while they tucked into the kebabs and thinking, this is exactly what it's all about – sharing food and having a laugh with your friends.

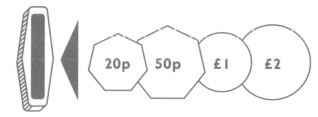

You can find a link to this playlist at
checkonpresents.co.uk

DANCING ON THE CEILING	DON'T STOP ME NOW
★ **LIONEL RICHIE** ★	☆ **QUEEN** ☆
EASY LOVER	PUSH IT
☆ **PHIL COLLINS** ☆	★ **SALT-N-PEPA** ★
(I'VE HAD) THE TIME OF MY LIFE	DON'T YOU WANT ME
★ **BILL MEDLEY AND JENNIFER WARNES** ★	☆ **THE HUMAN LEAGUE** ☆

★ PLAYLIST ★

GROOVE IS IN THE HEART	TINY DANCER
☆ **DEEE-LITE** ☆	★ **ELTON JOHN** ★
MO MONEY MO PROBLEMS	MAGGIE MAY
★ **THE NOTORIOUS B.I.G.** ★	☆ **ROD STEWART** ☆
BORDERLINE	WANTED DEAD OR ALIVE
☆ **MADONNA** ☆	★ **BON JOVI** ★

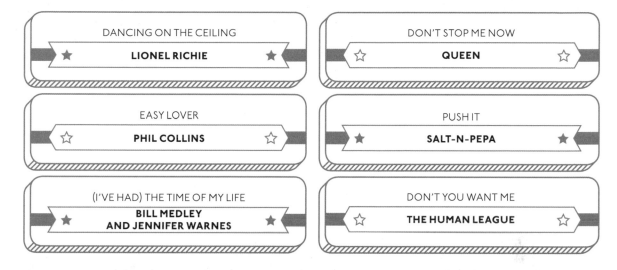
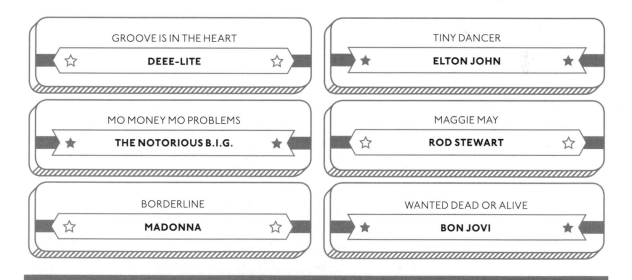

CHICKEN DONER KEBAB

GEORGE: When it comes to kebabs Terry loves lamb, but my favourite is chicken. It's just that bit easier to make and I love the smoky flavour the paprika brings to it. When we make these for parties, the chicken is usually the most popular...

SERVES 4–6

3 skinless chicken breasts
4 skinless and boneless
    chicken thighs

For the marinade
2 tbsp smoked paprika
1 tsp cayenne pepper
1 tsp freshly ground black pepper
1 tsp Cornish sea salt
50ml vegetable oil
Zest and juice of 1 lemon
3 garlic cloves, crushed

To serve
Warmed flatbreads or tortillas
1 iceberg lettuce, finely sliced
2 tomatoes, thinly sliced
Check On Chilli Sauce
    (see page 94)
Pickled Cucumber (see page 101)
Roasted Garlic Mayo
    (see page 47)
Toasted sesame seeds

1. Place the chicken and all the ingredients for the marinade in a large bowl and mix well. Cover with some cling film and pop into the fridge for a couple of hours to let the flavours infuse.

2. Preheat the oven to 180°C/ Gas 4. Remove the chicken from the fridge and let it come up to room temperature.

3. Tip the chicken into a large roasting tray and cook in the oven for 25 minutes until cooked through. Once cooked allow to rest for 10 minutes before chopping into small bite-sized pieces. Put into a serving bowl along with the cooking juices.

4. The best way to serve these is to pile everything on to the table and let your friends build their own kebabs, garnishing with whatever they want.

LAMB KEBAB WITH POMEGRANATE

TERRY: Right, this is it… I LOVE KEBABS… I feel like it's a confession, a weight off my chest, a dirty little secret that I've been ashamed to tell the world but it's out there now. It's my ultimate guilty pleasure. Imagine my surprise when George told me he'd never had one. I was shocked. No, I was appalled. This had to be rectified… six pints later and a trip to the local takeaway, his kebab virginity was gone and his life would never be the same again (well, not quite his life but definitely his waistline).

This is our version of the classic, using top-quality lamb and some great homemade sauces.

SERVES 6

Splash of vegetable oil
100g butter
3 onions, finely chopped
5 large garlic cloves,
   finely chopped
1.5kg minced lamb breast
2 tsp ground cumin
100g chopped fresh coriander
2 tsp fresh thyme leaves
Salt and freshly ground
   black pepper

To serve
Warmed flatbreads
   or pitta breads
1 iceberg lettuce, finely sliced
2 tomatoes, thinly sliced
Check On Chilli Sauce
   (see page 94)
Pickled Cucumber (see page 101)
Roasted Garlic Mayo
   (see page 47)
Seeds of 1 pomegranate

1. Put the oil and butter in a large, heavy-based pan and gently cook the onions and garlic over a low heat until soft and translucent. Once cooked, set aside and allow to cool completely.

2. Place the lamb, cumin, coriander and thyme in an extra-large bowl and season with salt and pepper. Mix well to combine, then fry about a teaspoon of the mixture in a small frying pan to check the seasoning.

3. Line a medium-sized roasting tin with parchment paper and add the lamb mixture, pressing down and tightly packing the mix into the tray. Cover the lamb with another roasting tin and top with a heavy ovenproof terrine mould or similar to 'press' the lamb. Place in the fridge for at least 3 hours.

4. Preheat the oven to 160°C/ Gas 3. Remove the weight from the lamb and put it, still in the roasting tin, in the oven. Cook for 35–40 minutes – if you have a meat thermometer, the centre of the meat should reach 65°C. Once cooked, allow to rest for 15–20 minutes before turning out and slicing into thick strips.

5. Place your lamb doner meat on a platter with the garnishes and let everyone crack on. Loads of chilli sauce for me, please! Finish with some fresh pomegranate seeds to add a burst of freshness.

CHECK ON CHILLI SAUCE

A good chilli sauce consists of the five 'S's: spicy, salty, sweet, savoury and sour. Our version is great as a marinade, on some scrambled eggs in the morning, and is also perfect on our kebabs.

400g fat red chillies
4 red peppers
16 garlic cloves
200ml rice wine vinegar
4 tbsp tomato purée
7 tbsp honey
4 tbsp fish sauce
2 tbsp soy sauce
Juice of 1 lime

1. Pop all the ingredients into a food processor and blitz for 10 minutes until completely smooth.

2. Pour into a pan and bring to the boil. Reduce the heat and simmer for 20–25 minutes, then remove from the heat and taste it to check it's how you like it. Add a little more of whatever you think it needs: if you think it's too spicy add some more honey, for example. It's all about personal taste, so don't be afraid to use your judgment.

3. Store in an airtight container in the fridge for up to 2 weeks.

FISH FINGERS AND CURRY SAUCE

TERRY: Between the ages of 8 and 10 this was all my little sister (see photo opposite... butter wouldn't melt!) would eat when we'd go out for dinner, which meant choosing a restaurant that would cater to her demands. I once offered to buy her the games console she wanted if she would eat some of my rare steak and béarnaise sauce... she point-blank refused. To be honest, I admired her resilience; she wanted that console more than anything in the world. This recipe is for her and her stubbornness – wouldn't change her for the world!

SERVES 4 (MAKES 12 FINGERS)

1kg cod fillet, skinned, pin-boned
    and cut into finger-sized strips
Flour, for dusting
2 eggs
100ml milk
200g panko breadcrumbs
100g crushed cornflakes
Salt and freshly ground
    black pepper
750ml vegetable oil
    for deep-frying
Thick-cut white bread, to serve

For the curry sauce
1 tbsp oil
4 large onions, chopped
6 garlic cloves, finely chopped
1 tsp fennel seeds
1 tsp cumin seeds
1 red chilli, chopped
2 cardamom pods
2 tsp medium curry powder
2.5cm piece of fresh ginger,
    chopped
2 large green apples, finely diced
2 litres vegetable stock
250ml coconut milk
Salt

1. Cut the cod into finger-sized strips. Season the flour and place in a shallow bowl. Beat the eggs and milk together in a separate bowl and put the breadcrumbs and cornflakes in another. Toss the cod strips in the seasoned flour, then the egg mix and finally the breadcrumb mix. Set aside while you make the curry sauce.

2. Heat the oil in a large pan and gently fry the onions, garlic, fennel and cumin seeds, chilli and cardamom over a medium heat until the onions are soft.

3. Add the curry powder, ginger and apples and cook for a further 5 minutes, then stir in the vegetable stock and simmer for about 25 minutes. Remove from the heat and leave to cool for 20–25 minutes before transferring to a blender and blitzing until smooth and thick. Stir in the coconut milk and set aside until

ready to serve (you will have more than you need for this recipe, but it's perfect for freezing into smaller batches and using as the base for any type of curry).

4. Heat the vegetable oil in a large, heavy-based pan or deep fryer to 180°C (drop a few of the breadcrumbs in to test that the oil is up to temperature). Fry the fingers in batches for 3–4 minutes, or until golden brown. Remove with a slotted spoon, drain on kitchen paper and season with salt to taste.

5. Serve the fish fingers with the curry sauce on the side to dip into. Thick-cut white bread is the absolute dream combo... fish finger sandwiches are where it's at!

THE ULTIMATE STEAK SANDWICH

GEORGE: The key to this EPIC sandwich is removing all the dough from inside the baguettes so you can stuff them full of tasty goodness. We made these a few months before our first pop-up round at Terry's house for the lads in my band. Unusually the room fell completely silent for about 10 minutes while everyone shut up and concentrated on eating!

SERVES 6

2 sirloin steaks, about 400g each
Splash of vegetable oil
2 onions, thinly sliced
4 large field mushrooms,
　　thickly sliced
2 large baguettes
English mustard, for spreading
Roasted Garlic Mayo
　　(see page 47), for spreading
500g rocket
Salt and freshly ground
　　black pepper

1. Season the steaks well with salt and pepper on both sides. Heat a splash of oil in a frying pan over a medium heat and fry the steaks for about 3–5 minutes on each side for medium rare. Remove from the pan and transfer to a board to rest for 5 minutes.

2. In the same pan, fry the onions and mushrooms over a high heat until cooked.

3. Cut each baguette into thirds and then slice lengthways. Remove the doughy centre from each baguette (this can be kept to make breadcrumbs).

4. Once the steaks have rested, trim away any fat and cut into thin slices. Use the baguette to mop up any juices from the chopping board – it's too delicious to waste!

5. Spread one side of each baguette with English mustard and the other with Roasted Garlic Mayo before topping with the fried onions and mushrooms, steak slices and rocket.

JALAPEÑO MAC AND CHEESE

When you pull this creamy, cheesy, bubbling dish of pure sin out of the oven, we swear to god you will burn your tongue because you can't wait to get it in your mouth! We've added some jalapeños to give it that extra kick. If you're a pro mac and cheese eater, you will fight to get the crunchy cheese bits around the edges. They're the BEST!

SERVES 6–8

500g macaroni
100g butter
100g flour
800ml full-fat milk
150ml double cream
1 tbsp English mustard
200g mature Cheddar, grated
200g Red Leicester, grated
4 egg yolks
150g jalapeños (from a jar),
    chopped

1. Preheat the oven to 180°C/Gas 4.

2. Cook the macaroni in a large pan of boiling salted water until al dente, or according to the packet instructions. Drain and refresh in cold water and set aside.

3. Melt the butter in a heavy-based pan over a medium heat and add the flour. Cook, stirring, until you have a smooth paste.

4. Heat the milk, cream and mustard in a separate pan over a low heat. Slowly add this mixture to the flour and butter, stirring all the time to avoid any lumps forming. Once it's all combined, add the grated cheeses and stir until melted and smooth. Finally stir in the egg yolks and jalapeños.

5. Combine the sauce with the macaroni and tip into an ovenproof dish. Bake in the oven for 25 minutes, until golden and bubbling at the edges.

PICKLES

TERRY: Pickling vegetables and fruit is an age-old way of preserving food. The one thing almost everyone will have tried will be pickled onions; for some people that sour twang of vinegar can be almost addictive. I'm a massive fan of pickling. The possibilities are endless – once you have a basic pickling liquor recipe you can experiment with whatever you like. The liquor takes on the flavour of whatever you are pickling – it's also great to use in salad dressings.

STRAIGHT-UP PICKLING LIQUOR

700ml white wine vinegar
400ml water
300g caster sugar
16 peppercorns
6 star anise
1 bay leaf
1 tsp fennel seeds
10 cloves

1. Place all the ingredients in a heavy-based pan and bring to the boil, then reduce the heat and simmer for 10 minutes.

2. Remove from the heat and allow to cool and infuse for an hour before straining into an airtight container. Store in the fridge until ready to use.

PICKLED PEACHES

These lovely sweet-and-sour-style peaches go brilliantly with rich, fatty meats such as roast belly pork, lamb and duck (see Roasted Duck Breast with Pickled Peaches and Celeriac, page 74). You'll find peaches with the best flavour in August.

5 peaches, halved
    and stones removed
800ml pickling liquor (see left)
5 thyme sprigs

1. Place the peach halves in a kilner jar or airtight container and add the pickling liquor and thyme sprigs.

2. Store in a cool, dark cupboard for at least 5 days before using.

GIN-PICKLED ONIONS

These are inspired by a classic gin martini garnished with cocktail onions. We serve them in martini glasses as a little snack at the bar, finished with a splash of great English gin.

500g baby silverskin onions
Rind of 1 lemon
5 thyme sprigs, plus extra
    to garnish
350ml gin
600ml pickling liquor (see left)

1. Place the onions in a large kilner jar or sealable container along with the lemon rind and thyme sprigs.

2. Pour over the pickling liquor and gin and leave to infuse for 2–3 days before serving.

3. Serve with some fresh thyme sprigs to garnish.

PICKLED CUCUMBER

These are best pickled quickly and are great with fish or lamb... light, fresh and crunchy!

1 cucumber, sliced into
    thin rounds
Pinch of sea salt
4 tbsp pickling liquor (see left)
Pinch of black sesame seeds

1. Pop the cucumber slices into a large bowl and season with a good pinch of sea salt. Mix thoroughly and set aside for 15 minutes for the salt to draw some of the moisture from the cucumber.

2. Use your hands to transfer the cucumber to a fresh bowl, discarding any liquid that has come out from the salting. Add the pickling liquor and mix. Leave to marinate for 20 minutes. Serve as a side dish, sprinkled with black sesame seeds.

BURNT SALTED CARAMEL ICE CREAM

As guilty pleasures go, ice cream is top of the list. It's the perfect dessert to round off a meal, or for just crashing out in front of the TV with a big bowl and an even bigger spoon. We make a really dark caramel so it's just burnt, which goes perfectly with the sweet ice cream. You'll need an ice cream machine for this recipe.

MAKES 2 LITRES

1 litre full-fat milk
750ml double cream
1 vanilla pod, slit lengthways
    and seeds scraped out
400g caster sugar
16 egg yolks*
Good pinch of sea salt

1. Gently warm the milk, cream and vanilla seeds in a heavy-based pan over a low heat.

2. Put the sugar into a separate heavy-based pan and place over a medium heat to slowly dissolve without stirring. When the sugar has turned to a dark brown caramel, slowly and carefully add the milk and cream. Take care, as the mixture will spit and bubble when it hits the hot caramel.

3. Whisk the egg yolks in a bowl for a few minutes until light and fluffy, then carefully add a ladle of the warm caramel cream, whisking all the time. Add the remaining caramel cream and return the pan to a low heat. Cook gently, stirring continuously, until the mixture is thick enough to coat the back of a spoon.

4. Remove from the heat and continue to stir for a further 5 minutes as it cools. Pass the mixture through a fine sieve. When the mixture has cooled completely, add a good pinch of sea salt.

5. Transfer to an ice cream machine and churn following the manufacturer's instructions.

* See page 246 for how to use up your leftover egg whites.

CHOCOLATE RICE PUDDING WITH TOASTED MARSHMALLOWS

There are two ways to make a rice pudding: on the stove top like this one or in the oven. Personally I'm not a big fan of the skin you get on the top when you bake rice pudding, plus I like to be able to taste it as I'm making it. You can create endless variations of this – bananas, raspberries – even sweets, which give a lovely chewy texture.

SERVES 4–6

1.5 litres full-fat milk
250ml double cream
50g caster sugar
250g pudding rice
1 vanilla pod
100g dark chocolate,
   roughly chopped
1 x 135g tin condensed milk
50g unsalted butter
Few marshmallows, to serve

1. Put the milk, cream, sugar, rice and split vanilla pod in a large, heavy-based pan and bring to a gentle simmer over a low-medium heat, stirring all the time. Cook until the rice is tender and has lost its bite.

2. Stir in the chopped chocolate and allow to cool slightly before stirring in the condensed milk and butter.

3. Transfer the rice pudding to a serving dish and top with the marshmallows. Use a blowtorch to toast them until melted and golden; alternatively place under a very hot grill for a few minutes.

BRAMBLE SNAKEBITE

This is our refined version of the half cider, half lager and blackcurrant cordial. We've made more of a cheeky cocktail with some fresh blackberries, some tart pear juice and a splash of boozy liqueur.

SERVES 4

100ml pear juice
150ml pear liqueur
10 blackberries, plus extra
   to garnish
2 brown sugar cubes
Ice
2 x 330ml bottles light beer

1. Place the pear juice, pear liqueur, blackberries and sugar cubes in a cocktail shaker with plenty of ice and shake hard for 30 seconds.

2. Strain into 4 glasses, top with the light beer and garnish with the extra blackberries. Enjoy immediately.

BEST BREAKFAST

SMOKED HADDOCK AND CRAYFISH CORNISH PASTIES

BAKED SALMON WITH SMASHED CUCUMBER AND BREAD SALAD

FISHCAKES WITH TARTARE SAUCE

**ROASTED PORK CHOPS WITH SAGE BUTTER
AND YORKSHIRE RHUBARB SAUCE**

STRAWBERRIES AND CREAM

CUP OF TEA

BEST BRITISH CHEESES

SALT AND PEPPER WATER BISCUITS

GEORGE'S MARVELLOUS MEDICINE

We've always been passionate about sourcing, cooking and eating great British food. This chapter is a celebration of ingredients that are the bedrock of this fine country and includes absolutely classic combinations such as pork chop with rhubarb and salmon and cucumber. British food often has a reputation for being stodgy, but we want to show you that this is definitely not the case. All these dishes are perfect for feeding a crowd too.

POP-UP EVENT

GREAT BRITISH CLASSICS

WHY NOT TRY...

Having a themed evening can be great fun. Without spending a lot of money you can add nice little touches. If you go for a Great British Classics theme, old Heinz baked beans cans, glass milk bottles and Tate & Lyle golden syrup pots are great for serving cutlery in or even fresh flowers.

TERRY: Great British Classics was our fourth pop-up event back in 2013. We saw this as a fitting opportunity to really showcase what we were capable of. The menu we created featured classics such as fish and chips and bacon and eggs, but they each had a Check On twist. We've always deliberately written very sparse descriptions of the dishes on our menus. We find diners are intrigued and excited by what's in store. It brings an element of surprise which adds to the lively atmosphere of our pop-up events.

We had a ploughman's lunch, which was a pressed terrine of ham hock with Lancashire cheese, pickled onion sauce and a quail's egg. The bacon and egg course was a play on a butty with a soft-boiled egg, ketchup jelly and toasted bread sauce. For dessert I created my version of Terry's Chocolate Orange, accompanied by George's Marvellous Medicine, a delicious alcoholic smoothie.

GEORGE: We were given the opportunity to host the pop-up in the private billiard room in the Sanderson hotel in London, a quintessentially British setting! It was also slightly different from previous pop-ups, which had been held in pubs and burger joints. I put on a three-piece suit and brought along my 60s Dansette vinyl record player, playing great British classics such as The Who, The Beatles, Pink Floyd and The Rolling Stones as our guests dined. This was also the first time I was out on the floor hosting, as we could finally afford to bring in a chef to assist Terry in the kitchen. The hotel chefs admittedly did jump in and help us out. It was a ten-course meal for forty people, which we hadn't done before. At the end of the night, when we realised we'd pulled it off, it felt incredibly rewarding and was really a game changer for Check On.

20p 50p £1 £2

You can find a link to this playlist at
checkonpresents.co.uk

HAPPY JACK	ALL RIGHT NOW
THE WHO ★ ★	☆ **FREE** ☆

TILL THERE WAS YOU	STAY WITH ME
☆ **THE BEATLES** ☆	★ **THE FACES** ★

THIS WILL BE OUR YEAR	I WANT TO BREAK FREE
★ **THE ZOMBIES** ★	☆ **QUEEN** ☆

★ **PLAYLIST** ★

THAT'S ENTERTAINMENT	MONEY
☆ **THE JAM** ☆	★ **PINK FLOYD** ★

SATISFACTION	GOOD TIMES BAD TIMES
★ **THE ROLLING STONES** ★	☆ **LED ZEPPELIN** ☆

WATERLOO SUNSET	CHILDREN OF THE REVOLUTION
☆ **THE KINKS** ☆	★ **T. REX** ★

BEST BREAKFAST

This is our Check On best breakfast. Pick and choose what you fancy and make it your own. If you've got friends or family over, serve up at the table, buffet style, and let everyone dig in. Bacon, hash browns, tomatoes and sausages can all be kept warm in the oven until you're ready to serve. Eggs can be fried at the last minute, and to save faffing about with toast – bring the toaster to the table and let people make their own!

BLOODY MARY BEANS

Here's our quick way to jazz up your standard tin of baked beans: add some Tabasco, Worcestershire sauce and a splash of vodka to taste.

BACON

Quality is key with bacon. We always go for a thick cut, but smoked or unsmoked is a matter of preference. Whack it under a hot grill until crispy and finish with a drizzle of maple syrup for a little sweetness.

EGGS

It always has to be fried eggs! The trick for perfect fried eggs is to use very fresh eggs and fry them slowly in a splash of olive oil in a good non-stick pan. Add a twist of freshly ground black pepper and cook until the whites are just set and the yolks still runny.

HASH BROWNS

You haven't had proper hash browns until you've ordered them in an American diner. Here's our recipe – simple but awesome.

SERVES 4

2 large potatoes, peeled
    and grated
1 small onion, grated
Salt and freshly ground
    black pepper
Butter for frying

Mix the grated potatoes and onion in a bowl and season with salt and pepper. Use your hands to squeeze out the excess water, then shape into patties. Fry in a little butter for about 10 minutes, until golden and crispy, turning once.

BAKED TOMATOES

The key to great tomatoes at breakfast is to bake them slowly so that the excess water from the tomatoes evaporates – the less water the more intense the flavour. You can prepare these a day or so in advance and they are also great in salads, sandwiches or with a juicy steak.

Preheat the oven to its lowest setting (90°C/Gas ¼). Halve some plum tomatoes and arrange on a baking tray. Add a thin slice of garlic to each tomato half. Season with sea salt and freshly ground black pepper, sprinkle over some fresh thyme leaves and bake in the oven overnight. Alternatively increase the oven temperature to 120°C/Gas ½ and bake for 2–3 hours, keeping an eye on them.

SAUSAGES

We love our classics; none of those apricot and Stilton sausages round our place. Keep it simple with some great quality pork sausages. Speak to your butcher and ask him what's best.

SMOKED HADDOCK AND CRAYFISH CORNISH PASTIES

This is our spin on 'Stargazy Pie', a fish pie from Cornwall using mackerel. The fishermen named it 'stargazy' as it traditionally has the fish heads popping out of the top of the pastry, gazing skywards. We make ours as little smoked haddock pasties for tasting menus and serve them in paper bags. When you open the bags at the table the smell is beautiful!

MAKES 6 LARGE PASTIES

For the pastry
650g plain flour
2 tsp salt
180g chilled butter, grated
250ml cold water
2 egg whites, beaten with
    a pinch of salt
2 egg yolks

For the filling
50g butter
1 onion, thinly sliced
1 leek, sliced into rounds
1 carrot, cut into 1cm dice
1 swede, peeled and cut
    into 1cm dice
600g undyed smoked haddock,
    skinned, pin-boned and cut
    into 2cm dice
400g cooked crayfish tails
1 large Maris Piper potato,
    peeled and cut into 1cm dice
2 tbsp wholegrain mustard
1 tsp freshly ground black pepper

1. First make the pastry. Put the salt and flour in a large bowl and mix well. Add the grated butter and rub in with your fingertips until you have a crumb-like mixture. Gradually add the water a little at a time, kneading all the time with your fingertips, until the mixture comes together into a dough (you may not need all the water). Knead for 5 minutes until soft and bouncy. Wrap the dough in cling film and chill in the fridge for 1½ hours.

2. Melt the butter in a heavy-based pan over a medium heat and add the onion, leek, carrot and swede. Cook gently for 5–8 minutes until the onions are soft. Allow the vegetables to cool completely before combining with all the remaining filling ingredients in a large bowl.

3. Preheat the oven to 180°C/Gas 4. Divide the pastry evenly into 6 balls and roll each one into a circle about the size of a medium dinner plate.

4. Divide the fish and vegetable mix between the 6 circles, arranging them in a line down the middle. Brush the edges with the beaten egg white, then gently fold up the edges and press together. Lift on to a non-stick baking tray and brush the pasties all over with the egg yolks to glaze. Bake in the oven for about 30 minutes, or until golden.

5. Allow to rest for 10–15 minutes until cool enough to eat. Be warned: you WILL burn your mouth if you don't wait!

BAKED SALMON WITH SMASHED CUCUMBER AND BREAD SALAD

There is something quintessentially British about salmon and cucumber sandwiches. They just scream old-fashioned English picnic. We've updated them here with lightly baked salmon coated in soft herbs and a fresh cucumber and bread salad... definitely one to share with friends in the garden on a summer's day.

SERVES 6

2.5kg whole salmon fillet, pin-boned
3 tbsp English mustard
1 tsp malt vinegar
3 tbsp freshly chopped mint leaves
3 tbsp freshly chopped tarragon
3 tbsp freshly chopped parsley
Sea salt and freshly ground black pepper

For the salad

2 beef tomatoes
2 large cucumbers, chopped into chunky rounds
1 red onion, very thinly sliced
500g sourdough bread, torn into chunks
2 tbsp freshly chopped dill
1 red chilli, finely sliced
1 tsp sugar
1 tsp sea salt
1 tsp freshly ground black pepper

1. Preheat the oven to 160°C/ Gas 3 and line a large baking tray with parchment paper.

2. Lay the salmon fillet skin side down on the tray. Combine the English mustard and malt vinegar and brush on to the salmon fillet.

3. Mix the herbs and salt and pepper together in a bowl until thoroughly combined, then cover the top of the salmon with this herb mix, pressing to coat in an even layer. Cook the salmon in the oven for about 20 minutes, until just cooked. Remove from the oven and allow to rest.

4. Meanwhile make the salad. Take a large Tupperware container and roughly tear the tomatoes into it with your hands, giving them a really good squeeze. Add the remaining ingredients and seal the container, then proceed to give it a good hard shake for 60 seconds – the cucumber will be bashed around and the bread will absorb some of the juice. Set aside for 10 minutes to let the flavours infuse before serving with the salmon.

FISHCAKES WITH TARTARE SAUCE

TERRY: Bring back these truly wonderful things! We love fishcakes and don't think they get the praise they deserve. I think everyone loves a classic fishcake but no one makes them – they have been edged off menus across the country to make way for the now standard Thai crab cake with sweet chilli sauce. I almost feel sorry for them.

These lovely, crispy, fragrant fishcakes are easy peasy to make and are ready for a comeback.

SERVES 4

800g floury potatoes (such as Maris Piper), peeled and cut into chunks
300ml full-fat milk
1 bay leaf
400g undyed smoked haddock, roughly diced
1 shallot, finely diced
1 tbsp horseradish sauce
½ tsp wholegrain mustard
Zest and juice of 1 lemon
2 tbsp freshly chopped parsley
Plain flour, for dusting
2 eggs, lightly beaten
100g breadcrumbs (use panko if you can get hold of them)
100ml sunflower oil, for frying
Salt and freshly ground black pepper

For the tartare sauce

1 tbsp mayonnaise (see page 46)
30g finely diced shallot
30g finely chopped parsley, stalks removed
30g finely chopped gherkins
30g chopped capers

1. Cook the potatoes in boiling salted water until tender. Meanwhile pour the milk into a pan with the bay leaf and a pinch of salt and bring to a simmer. Add the haddock and remove from the heat. Set aside to cool.

2. Drain the cooked potatoes thoroughly and put through a potato ricer or mash until smooth.

3. In a large bowl, combine the potatoes with the finely diced shallot, horseradish, mustard, lemon zest and juice and parsley. Remove the haddock from the milk with a slotted spoon and gently fold into the potato mixture. Season to taste with salt and pepper.

4. Allow to cool before shaping into 8 patties. Chill in the fridge for 30 minutes while you combine all the ingredients for the tartare sauce in a small bowl.

5. Lightly flour the patties and dip each one in the beaten egg and then in the breadcrumbs. Heat the oil in a large frying pan and fry the fishcakes (in batches) over a medium heat for about 5 minutes on each side, or until golden. Serve immediately, with the tartare sauce.

ROASTED PORK CHOPS WITH SAGE BUTTER AND YORKSHIRE RHUBARB SAUCE

GEORGE: Whenever we head to Yorkshire to stay at my mum's house we almost always pay a visit to the Ginger Pig farm, where the happiest pigs in Yorkshire are reared. It's such a beautiful drive through the moors – Yorkshire is truly my favourite place on earth and has some of the best produce in the country and obviously the best rhubarb in the world. We always have this for dinner when we're up North. It's Yorkshire on a plate, in all its glory!

SERVES 4

4 large pork chops,
    about 300g each
Oil, for rubbing
150g butter
8 sage leaves
2 tbsp cider vinegar
Salt and freshly ground
    black pepper

For the rhubarb sauce
300g rhubarb, chopped
80g caster sugar
100g cold butter, diced

1. Preheat the oven to 180°C/Gas 4.

2. First make the sauce. Place the rhubarb, sugar and a splash of water in a heavy-based pan and cook gently over a low-medium heat until the rhubarb is soft. Remove from the heat and blitz in a blender until smooth and thick. Pass through a fine sieve into a clean pan and set aside until ready to serve.

3. Place a frying pan over a medium heat while you score or snip off the fatty rind of the chops. Rub the chops with a little oil and season with salt and pepper. Brown the chops two at a time for 4–6 minutes on each side, depending on their thickness. Transfer the chops to a baking tray and finish in the oven for a further 8 minutes.

4. Meanwhile, in the same pan that you used to brown the chops, cook the butter and sage leaves for a few minutes until golden before adding the cider vinegar. Set aside.

5. When you are ready to serve, warm the rhubarb sauce and beat in the cold diced butter. Spoon the brown butter and sage over the chops and serve with the warm rhubarb sauce on the side.

STRAWBERRIES AND CREAM

TERRY: There's not a single doubt in my mind that British strawberries are the best in the entire world. Every summer we have these beauties, right on our doorsteps, so much so that I can't ever contemplate buying imported out-of-season strawberries – they don't even come close to the flavour. I try to leave them alone as much as possible but can't resist them with this cinnamon cream.

SERVES 4

400g British strawberries
300ml double cream
1 tsp ground cinnamon,
   or to taste

1. Buy the best British strawberries that you can.

2. Whip the double cream lightly until soft peaks form. Stir in the ground cinnamon, adding more to taste if you wish.

3. Serve the strawberries with dollops of the soft cinnamon cream.

CUP OF TEA

The British Empire was built on cups of tea, but you won't have seen one like this before! This cuppa will cool you down on a hot summer's day. It's perfect served with some sugary biscuits but also makes a great dessert that can be made well in advance and finished off with a spoon of vanilla-scented Chantilly cream.

SERVES 4

8 Earl Grey tea bags
650ml boiling water
7 sheets of leaf gelatine
Juice of 1 lemon
150g caster sugar
Shop bought biscuits or
    Ginger Snaps, to serve
    (for recipe see page 177)

For the Chantilly cream
150ml whipping cream
1 vanilla pod, slit lengthways
1 tbsp icing sugar

1. Place the tea bags in a large heatproof jug and pour the boiling water on top. Leave the tea to steep for 30 minutes, then remove the tea bags.

2. Meanwhile place the gelatine sheets in a small bowl of cold water and leave to soften for a few minutes.

3. Squeeze out the excess water from the gelatine sheets and add to the tea along with the lemon juice and sugar; stir until dissolved. Pour into teacups and leave to set for at least 3 hours.

4. When you are ready to serve, whip the cream until soft peaks form. Scrape the seeds from the vanilla pod and add to the cream, along with the icing sugar.

5. Serve the 'tea' with the Chantilly cream and biscuits or crisp Ginger Snaps.

BEST BRITISH CHEESES

These days there's more to British cheese than Cheddar and Stilton.
These are some of our favourite cheeses being made in Britain today.

BLUE MONDAY

This soft ivory white cheese with purple blue streaks is made in Yorkshire and was originally produced for Blur bass guitarist Alex James, who named it after his favourite song by Manchester band New Order. Perfect melted on a burger, toasted with some green beans or simply spread on some warm sourdough toast.

MRS KIRKHAM'S LANCASHIRE

This rich, buttery, crumbly-textured cow's milk cheese is a real pleasure to eat and is great for making fondues. It's got a hint of sharpness that goes well with earthy beetroots.

TUNWORTH

A sexy, soft, gooey cheese – perfect for popping in the oven and getting dippy with. It's got a distinct nutty flavour with a hint of mushroomy goodness. It lends itself well to soft herbs and crunchy vegetables.

HOMEWOOD HALLOUMI

Yep, British halloumi made in Somerset. We absolutely love the salty goodness this has to offer. Great just pan-fried with some oven-baked tomatoes and good-quality rapeseed oil.

BERKSWELL

A hard ewe's milk cheese with a salty, intense flavour that varies with the season of production, we love to use this instead of Parmesan. It's really great shaved with a peeler over dressed tomatoes or finely grated over spaghetti and meatballs.

SALT AND PEPPER WATER BISCUITS

These simple-to-make, rustic style biscuits are a great accompaniment to all types of cheese. Most people expect to see shop-bought crackers with the cheese board, so it's always a nice personal touch to bring out these homemade savoury biscuits.

MAKES 18–20 BISCUITS

230g plain flour
1 tsp baking powder
50g chilled butter, cubed
5 tbsp ice-cold water
Pinch of sea salt
Few grinds of black pepper

1. Preheat the oven to 180°C/Gas 4 and line a couple of baking sheets with parchment paper.

2. Put the flour, baking powder and butter in a food processor and whizz until the mixture resembles rough crumbs. Add the water and work in, just to bring the mixture together to form a dough.

3. Turn the dough out onto a floured surface and roll out as thinly as possible, into a neat rectangle. Brush the surface with a little water and season with salt and pepper. Prick the dough all over with a fork, then cut into squares.

4. Place the squares on the lined trays and bake in the oven for 10–15 minutes, or until the biscuits are cooked but are still pale. Transfer to a wire rack and leave until completely cool. These will keep in an airtight container for up to 2 weeks.

GEORGE'S MARVELLOUS MEDICINE

The title for this is inspired by the classic Roald Dahl story, although we can promise that it will taste a lot better and, although marvellous, won't have quite the same effect! It's essentially an alcoholic smoothie and is a great combination of dessert and after-dinner liqueur. Definitely not one for the kids. We like to serve this in little milk bottles with straws.

SERVES 4-6

100g fresh blueberries
100g fresh blackberries
3 large scoops of ice cream
150g full-fat milk
100ml Pernod
Ice, to serve

1. Place all the ingredients in a blender and blitz until smooth.

2. Serve immediately over ice.

GRILLED SCALLOPS WITH BACON BUTTER

GRILLED PRAWN COCKTAIL BURGERS

MACKEREL HOT DOGS WITH FRESH TOMATO AND CHILLI SALSA

POOR MAN'S POTATOES

HERITAGE TOMATO, RED ONION AND TARRAGON SALAD

BONED LEG OF LAMB WITH ROSEMARY AND MINT

LAMB CHOP DIB DABS

SALAD DRESSINGS

BARBECUED RUM-MARINATED PINEAPPLE WITH TOFFEE SAUCE

G&T ICE LOLLIES

LAGERITAS

There's no denying it: at the first sign of summer sun, our first thought is to get the barbecue fired up. There's something special about relaxing in the sun and cooking outdoors that is just pure bliss. If there is one way to bring people together over food then this is definitely it. In this chapter we've put together a selection of recipes that are perfect for barbecuing – boned leg of lamb with rosemary and mint served with our tomato and tarragon salad, mackerel hot dogs and prawn cocktail burgers, all washed down with a pitcher of lageritas. So text your mates and tell them to come over with a bottle of something cold.

POP-UP EVENT

A VERY BRITISH BARBECUE

WHY NOT TRY...

Prepare as much in advance as you can: marinate any meat overnight, make salads that improve at room temperature (such as our tomato and tarragon salad) rather than wilt in the sun, and set up a table outside where you can serve up the dishes and everyone can help themselves.

GEORGE: It was the good old summer barbecue that inspired us to put on one of our pop-up events. We found an amazing open roof space and to create a bit of a buzz we offered 150 free tickets.

I remember lugging giant bags of ice up to the top of the roof space – having plenty of ice is ESSENTIAL. No one wants a warm beer or glass of Prosecco!

We had a huge turnout, which led to an incredible atmosphere. I jumped on the decks and played some songs – everything from The Kinks 'Sunny Afternoon' to DJ Jazzy Jeff & The Fresh Prince's 'Summertime'!

TERRY: We wanted to give people a great barbecue that was a bit different from the usual burgers and sausages (not that there is anything wrong with those!). We wanted fresh, summery flavours and so we came up with mackerel hot dogs, which went down a storm. We also cooked over 100 scallops straight on the grill in their shells, which we then finished with bacon butter. Everyone absolutely loved these so we've included the recipe for you in this chapter.

If you're cooking on coals, make sure you give yourself plenty of time to light them up (about half an hour). Wait until the flames die down and the coals are turning white – that's when you know it's time to start cooking.

When it comes to hosting a party, bringing people together over some food and cocktails, nothing beats a barbecue… Check On style.

You can find a link to this playlist at
checkonpresents.co.uk

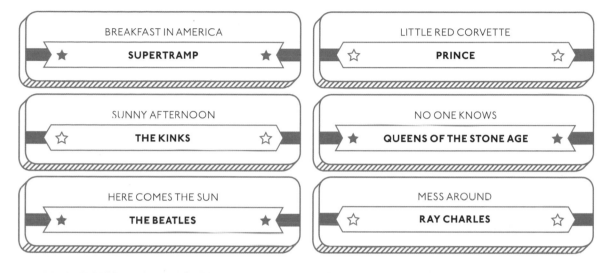

BREAKFAST IN AMERICA
★ **SUPERTRAMP** ★

LITTLE RED CORVETTE
☆ **PRINCE** ☆

SUNNY AFTERNOON
☆ **THE KINKS** ☆

NO ONE KNOWS
★ **QUEENS OF THE STONE AGE** ★

HERE COMES THE SUN
★ **THE BEATLES** ★

MESS AROUND
☆ **RAY CHARLES** ☆

PLAYLIST

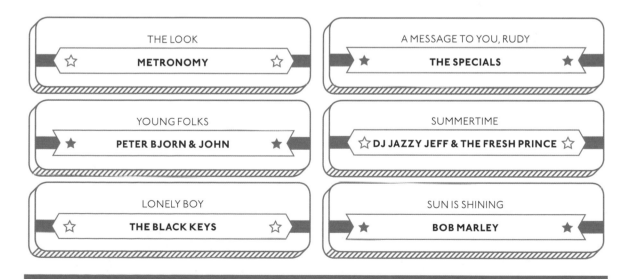

THE LOOK
☆ **METRONOMY** ☆

A MESSAGE TO YOU, RUDY
★ **THE SPECIALS** ★

YOUNG FOLKS
★ **PETER BJORN & JOHN** ★

SUMMERTIME
☆ **DJ JAZZY JEFF & THE FRESH PRINCE** ☆

LONELY BOY
☆ **THE BLACK KEYS** ☆

SUN IS SHINING
★ **BOB MARLEY** ★

GRILLED SCALLOPS WITH BACON BUTTER

Ask your fishmonger for hand-dived scallops; they are a thing of absolute beauty. They will usually be bigger, cleaner and a lot better for the seabed than dredged scallops. All you really need to do is give them a quick wash and they are pretty much good to go.

SERVES 8

8 large scallops from your local
    fishmonger, each still attached
    in a half shell
Splash of rapeseed oil
Juice of ½ lemon
1 tsp chopped parsley
Sea salt and freshly ground
    black pepper

For the bacon butter*
10 rashers of smoked
    streaky bacon
250g unsalted butter

1. First make the bacon butter. Cook the bacon slowly in a frying pan until it is super crispy, then remove from the pan and allow to cool. Place in a blender with the frying fat and blitz until you have coarse crumbs. Add the butter and blitz again until well mixed.

2. Remove the butter and roll into a cylinder. Wrap in cling film and chill in the fridge for about 30 minutes. Slice the butter into thin rounds.

3. Preheat a grill to high. Oil and season the scallops, then place them under the grill and cook for 1–2 minutes. Turn the scallops over, add a thin round of bacon butter and return to the grill for a further minute.

4. Carefully remove from the grill and allow to cool for a minute or so before serving – the shells will be very hot!

5. Finish with a squeeze of lemon juice and a sprinkle of chopped parsley on each scallop.

* This bacon butter is great spread on toast in the morning.

GRILLED PRAWN COCKTAIL BURGERS

TERRY: When I first mentioned this burger to George, he gave me a look that I've come to know very well... it's the 'calm down Terry, you're getting carried away fella' look. But once I had made it, he was converted (which is usually the case). It's a play on a classic prawn cocktail.

Cook it, eat it and make your own mind up... I'm pretty sure you'll love it too!

MAKES 6 LARGE BURGERS OR 10 SLIDERS

1 tbsp olive oil,
    plus extra for grilling
1 large onion, finely diced
2 garlic cloves, finely chopped
1 carrot, finely diced
2 tsp cayenne pepper
1 tsp smoked paprika
Zest and juice of 1 lemon
1kg jumbo prawn tails, peeled
2 tbsp soft white breadcrumbs
Salt and freshly ground
    black pepper

For the cocktail sauce
75g mayonnaise
75g ketchup
Tabasco, to taste
15ml brandy
Splash of Worcestershire sauce
1/2 tsp smoked paprika

To serve
6 brioche buns (or 10 mini ones)
Baby Gem lettuce leaves
Sliced beef tomato
Pickled Cucumber (see page 101)

1. Heat the oil in a pan and gently sweat the onion, garlic and carrot over a low-medium heat for about 10 minutes, until the onions are soft. Transfer to a bowl to cool completely and then add the cayenne, paprika and lemon zest and juice.

2. Place the prawn tails in a food processor with the cooled vegetables and breadcrumbs and blitz to a coarse mixture. Season with salt and pepper. Fry a small amount of the mixture so you can taste and adjust the seasoning if necessary.

3. Divide and shape the mixture into 6 flattened patties and chill in the fridge for 30 minutes while you prepare the sauce.

4. Combine all the sauce ingredients together in a bowl; taste and adjust the seasoning and set aside until ready to serve. (If you have a squeezy bottle, pour the sauce into one of these.)

5. Lightly oil both sides of each patty and place on the hottest part of the barbecue for 2 minutes on each side, turning carefully. Then move over to a cooler part of the barbecue for another 8–10 minutes, turning halfway through cooking.

6. Spread (or squirt) both sides of the brioche buns with the cocktail sauce and assemble the burgers with lettuce, tomato slices and Pickled Cucumber.

MACKEREL HOT DOGS WITH FRESH TOMATO AND CHILLI SALSA

Once you've tried this fishy delight, it'll become a staple of your summer... spicy barbecued fish with fresh tomato and chilli salsa has to be a winner in anyone's book. Any leftover salsa makes a great dip for corn chips or dolloped on to a cheeseburger.

SERVES 8

8 mackerel fillets, v-cut
   and pin-boned
1 tbsp harissa paste
Good pinch of salt
8 brioche hot dog buns

For the salsa

10 plum tomatoes, deseeded
   and diced
2 red chillies, deseeded and
   finely diced
2 banana shallots, finely diced
3 tbsp chives
3 spring onions, very finely sliced
1 tsp honey
2 tbsp sherry vinegar
1 tsp sea salt

1. To make the salsa, place all the ingredients in a bowl and mix well. Taste and adjust the seasoning: if you like a little more heat, add some more chilli; if you feel like it needs a grind of pepper, go for it. Set aside for at least 20 minutes to let the flavours infuse.

2. Lightly rub the mackerel fillets all over with the harissa paste and a pinch of salt.

3. Place the mackerel fillets skin side down on a hot barbecue and cook, without turning, for about 7–10 minutes. Alternatively you can place them under a grill preheated to high and cook for 5–7 minutes.

4. Split the brioche buns and warm for a minute or two on the barbecue. Pop a mackerel fillet into each one and top with the salsa.

POOR MAN'S POTATOES

TERRY: This is a lovely, simple Spanish dish that I've been eating for years and years on family holidays. I was an absolute nightmare eater as a kid – the definitive ham, egg and chips English tourist. Thankfully that all changed, but back then this was a staple of my holiday diet. It's a great barbecue side and a dish you can make in advance.

Don't be alarmed by the amount of oil used here – once cooled you can strain it and use it again.

SERVES 6–8

8 large Maris Piper potatoes,
    peeled and cut into 1cm slices
10 garlic cloves, sliced
8 thyme sprigs
Tiny pinch of saffron
1 tbsp sea salt
750ml best-quality olive oil
    (preferably Spanish)

1. Preheat the oven to 130°C/Gas 1.

2. Place the potato slices in a large roasting tin with the garlic, thyme, saffron and salt and mix thoroughly with your hands.

3. Pour over the olive oil – it should completely cover the potatoes. Cook the potatoes in the oven for 30–40 minutes until tender.

4. Remove the potatoes and garlic slices from the pan using a slotted spoon and serve immediately. Allow the oil to cool completely before straining through a sieve to reuse.

HERITAGE TOMATO, RED ONION AND TARRAGON SALAD

It's all about the tomatoes in this recipe! If you can get hold of some great tomatoes they really don't need much: a bit of salt and pepper, rapeseed oil and some tarragon is all you need. The juice from the tomatoes creates its own dressing.

SERVES 6–8

3kg heritage tomatoes, or
　　the best tomatoes you can find
1 red onion, finely sliced
1 bunch of fresh tarragon,
　　leaves picked
Splash of rapeseed oil
Sea salt and freshly ground
　　black pepper

1. Roughly chop the tomatoes into bite-sized chunks and pop into a large bowl with the sliced red onion, picked tarragon leaves and a splash of oil. Season generously with salt and pepper and gently toss the salad.

2. Taste and adjust the seasoning before serving.

BONED LEG OF LAMB WITH ROSEMARY AND MINT

TERRY: This is one of my all-time favourites. Lamb leg is such a lovely cut of meat but it can be an absolute pain to get an even pink colour when cooking on the bone; plus it's awkward to carve (although if you're carving then you do get first pick on the lovely flame-licked end pieces).

If it's lashing down with rain outside, just preheat the oven to 180°C/Gas 4 and pop the lamb on to a roasting rack with a tray underneath and a splash of water to collect the roasting juices. Cook for about 30 minutes until pink in the middle.

SERVES 6–8

1 boned leg of lamb, about 2 kg
5 garlic cloves
Handful of fresh mint,
    leaves picked
5 rosemary sprigs,
    leaves finely chopped
1 tbsp Dijon mustard
Good splash of rapeseed oil
Zest of 3 lemons
Salt and freshly ground
    black pepper

For the parsley salad
3 banana shallots,
    sliced into rings
4 tbsp capers, roughly chopped
1 tbsp white wine vinegar
2 tbsp lamb resting juices
3 large bunches of parsley,
    leaves picked
Bunch of fresh mint,
    leaves chopped

1. Lay your boned leg out on a chopping board and slash the meat several times in the thickest part. This will help cook the lamb evenly and also allow the marinade to get into the meat.

2. Use a pestle and mortar to grind the garlic, mint, rosemary, mustard, rapeseed oil, lemon zest, salt and pepper to a smooth paste. Rub into the lamb and leave to marinate in the fridge for at least 3 hours.

3. Remove the lamb from the fridge and allow to come to room temperature at least 30–40 minutes before you want to cook. Place on a barbecue rack on the highest position (furthest from the coals) and cook for about 15–20 minutes on each side, until the lamb is nice and pink in the middle. Allow to rest for 10 minutes on a plate to catch the beautiful resting juices.

4. While the lamb is resting, make the salad. Combine the shallots, capers, white wine vinegar and lamb resting juices and mix thoroughly. Stir the herbs into the dressing and serve with the sliced lamb.

LAMB CHOP DIB DABS

Remember eating sherbet dib dabs as a kid? Well, this is the meaty grown-up version. It's perfect for a barbecue, as you can pick up a beer in one hand and a chop in the other... caveman style! You can never have too many of these. We guarantee they will be a hit.

SERVES 5

10 lamb cutlets
Oil, for rubbing
Sea salt and freshly ground
    black pepper

For the dip
250g Greek yoghurt
Zest and juice of 1 lemon
2 tsp harissa paste
1 tbsp olive oil

For the crumbs
300g toasted hazelnuts
100g toasted flaked almonds
5 slices of white bread
2 tbsp fresh thyme leaves
1 tbsp freshly ground
    black pepper

1. Make the dip by combining all the ingredients together in a bowl. Set aside in the fridge until needed.

2. Place the crumb ingredients in a food processor and blitz until you have coarse crumbs. Tip into a bowl.

3. Trim away some of the excess fat from the chops (a little fat is great but you don't want too much). Lightly oil the chops and season with salt and pepper.

4. Cook the chops on a hot barbecue (or under a medium grill) for 3–4 minutes on each side. Serve with the dip and crumbs and get dipping!

SALAD DRESSINGS

These are super easy, and we always save old jars to make and store them in. They keep for a couple of weeks in the fridge. Just shake and go.

QUICK VINAIGRETTE

210ml best-quality olive oil
70ml cider vinegar
Salt and freshly ground
    black pepper

BUTTERMILK AND CHIVE

1 quantity of Quick Vinaigrette
    (see left)
70ml buttermilk
2 tbsp finely chopped chives

POMEGRANATE AND CHILLI

1 quantity of Quick Vinaigrette
    (see left)
1 fresh red chilli, deseeded
    and finely chopped
1 tbsp fresh pomegranate seeds
1 tsp pomegranate molasses

CHECK ON HOUSE DRESSING

1 quantity of Quick Vinaigrette
    (see left)
1 tsp wholegrain mustard
1 tsp garlic purée
1 tbsp natural yoghurt

BACON AND BLUE CHEESE

1 quantity of Quick Vinaigrette
    (see left)
2 tbsp chopped crispy
    smoked bacon
100g blue cheese,
    finely crumbled

BARBECUED RUM-MARINATED PINEAPPLE WITH TOFFEE SAUCE

Pineapple lends itself brilliantly to barbecuing. It's firm enough to withstand the heat and is super juicy and full of natural sugar – you should be able to get some lovely griddle marks when the sugar caramelises. In this recipe the dark rum gives the pineapple a lovely warmth.

If you're tight on barbecue space you can also pan-fry this on the hob (or use a griddle pan).

SERVES 6–8

2 fresh pineapples
200ml dark rum
200g soft dark brown sugar
100g butter
200ml double cream

1. Use a large, sharp knife to cut the skin off the pineapple, following the contours of the fruit. Slice into rounds about 2cm thick and remove the cores. Arrange in a large shallow dish, pour over the rum and scatter over 70g of the sugar. Leave to marinate for at least 5 hours, turning the slices and spooning over the rum every couple of hours.

2. When the coals are hot on your barbecue, remove the pineapple from the rum and sugar and barbecue for 2–3 minutes on each side, until the natural sugars start to caramelise.

3. For the toffee sauce, gently melt the remaining sugar in a pan, allowing it to cook to a golden caramel. Add the butter and double cream and stir until combined, then add the leftover marinade. Serve the pineapple warm, with the toffee sauce on the side.

G&T ICE LOLLIES

GEORGE: As you can see I'm dressed as a baby convict here, thanks for that nan! Chewing on that wooden rattle isn't half as tasty as these G&T ice lollies, perfect to cool you down in the sunshine. Plus they've got gin in, cheeky!

This is a playful dessert that can be handed out for people to munch on as they are chatting away. We don't know about your barbecues, but at ours once the food has been eaten and the sun starts to go down, the music gets turned up. That's when the party gets started – these are perfect for the transition.

MAKES 6

40g granulated sugar
50ml water
80ml gin
500ml tonic water
50ml fresh lemon juice

1. Place the sugar and water in a small pan over a low heat and stir until the sugar has melted. Allow to cool before combining with the gin, tonic water and lemon juice; stir well.

2. Pour into lolly moulds and place in the freezer.

LAGERITAS

GEORGE: This is an absolutely top-notch drink to cool your mouth down after some spicy wings or a lamb doner smothered in chilli sauce. I always keep a couple of glasses in the freezer at home for serving up frosty beers – you'd be surprised what a difference a chilled glass makes here.

SERVES 4

100ml fresh lime juice
200ml good-quality tequila
50ml Cointreau
4 x 330ml bottles Mexican beer
lime wedges, to serve

1. Shake the lime juice, tequila and Cointreau over ice for about 30 seconds.

2. Strain into chilled, salt-rimmed glasses and top with beer. Serve each glass with a wedge of lime.

CRISPY BELLY OF PORK WITH ROASTED ONIONS AND SAGE JUICES

SIRLOIN OF BEEF WITH HERBY HORSERADISH CRUST
AND PROPER ROASTING GRAVY

PERFECT ROAST POTATOES

ROASTED SQUASH WITH GORGONZOLA AND BASIL

PEAS WITH BACON AND LETTUCE

SALT-BAKED VEGETABLES

APRICOT AND PISTACHIO STUFFING

CAULIFLOWER CHEESE

YORKSHIRE PUDDING

TERRY'S CHOCOLATE ORANGE MOUSSE WITH GINGER SNAP CRUMBLE

ROASTED PLUMS WITH PECAN NUT CRUMBLE

SUNDAY DRINKING

The great British Sunday roast is all about family for us, when the third and fourth generations get round a table and eat the same meal they've been eating on a Sunday all their lives. It's special, as the trip often involves heading home to a parent's house or the grandparents to catch up. It doesn't matter whether you're coming home from university, back from serving in the army or just walking round the corner, the journey is always worth it. For us, living away from our families up North, recreating those Sunday dinners with our friends is the next best thing.

Here we've got George's taste of home with his mum's Yorkshire pudding recipe, and my recipe for apricot and pistachio stuffing, which reminds me of my mum always using packets of Paxo... (sorry Mum x).

POP-UP EVENT
SUNDAY DINNERS

WHY NOT TRY...

Sunday dinners are probably the epitome of relaxed eating. You want your friends and family to feel they can kick off their shoes and chill out on the sofa. Throw a pile of Sunday papers and magazines on a table for people to flick through while they're waiting for the roast to be ready.

TERRY: We could never have anticipated how popular these would be: we sold out every single Sunday, TWICE! (a sitting for 70 at 1 p.m. and the same again at 5 p.m.). It was our busiest ever time and we loved every second of it. It seems that everyone has a soft spot for Sunday lunch. Every Saturday we'd get into the venue – the Dead Dolls House in Shoreditch – carrying over 100kg of peeled potatoes in bags full of water into the kitchen…

looking back I can't believe we did it! Each Sunday was a different theme – chicken, beef or pork with the roast as the main course. We always like to have an element of surprise, so for the beef roast, the first course was Comté cheese fingers, which we served up in little boxes with a chilli dip. The second course was 'beef leaves' – a lovely combination of finely chopped quality beef sirloin and pickled vegetables served in Little Gem lettuce leaves. For dessert, we

went all out with a rich chocolate cake, chocolate mousse and a chocolate milk served in glass bottles. We dressed the room with plenty of candles to give it a lovely intimate feel and served the roasties and vegetables sharing style in large enamel dishes. We also served the gravy up in teapots, which went down a treat and again brought the 'comforts of home' vibe to the meal.

GEORGE: We really wanted a homely feel to our Sunday Dinner pop-ups. I started to put together the playlist, bringing together a collection of songs that Terry and I listen to on Sunday afternoons, while we're cooking a roast. It was essentially an eclectic mix of chilled-out tunes, including classics such as Lou Reed's 'Perfect Day' and Lionel Richie's 'Easy Like Sunday Morning'. We wanted to include the songs that we'd both grown up listening to, which for us really brought together the theme of family and music over Sunday dinners. Every time I listen to The Kinks it takes me back to Sunday dinner with my family, my mum cooking an amazing roast chicken and my dad getting his record collection out. When I was a kid I always thought that the albums he played were just 'dad music.' How wrong was I… all of my dad's favourite bands are now mine too.

20p 50p £1 £2

You can find a link to this playlist at
checkonpresents.co.uk

(SITTIN' ON) THE DOCK OF THE BAY	STRANGE THINGS
★ **OTIS REDDING** ★	☆ **RANDY NEWMAN** ☆

EASY LIKE SUNDAY MORNING	YOU CAN'T HIDE A LIGHT WITH THE DARK
☆ **LIONEL RICHIE** ☆	★ **BILL RYDER-JONES** ★

PERFECT DAY	RAPPER'S DELIGHT
★ **LOU REED** ★	☆ **THE SUGARHILL GANG** ☆

★ PLAYLIST ★

GEORGIA	DANCING IN THE MOONLIGHT
☆ **RAY CHARLES** ☆	★ **THIN LIZZY** ★

FAST CAR	LIFE IS A ROLLERCOASTER
★ **TRACY CHAPMAN** ★	☆ **RONAN KEATING** ☆

SINNERMAN	I CAN SEE CLEARLY NOW
☆ **NINA SIMONE** ☆	★ **JIMMY CLIFF** ★

CRISPY BELLY OF PORK WITH ROASTED ONIONS AND SAGE JUICES

This is a great marriage of flavours. Pork and sage are like Ant and Dec – perfect together! It's a great one-pot dish and with the sliced onions cooking underneath the pork and absorbing all those lovely roasting juices, you're on to a winner flavour-wise... oh, and let's not forget about the salty CRACKLING!

SERVES 6

2kg pork belly, boned
1 tbsp vegetable oil
2 carrots, peeled
2 celery sticks, trimmed
6 large onions, thinly sliced
10 large sage leaves,
    finely chopped
2 tbsp fresh thyme leaves
300ml cloudy apple juice
Sea salt and freshly ground
    black pepper

1. Preheat the oven to 160°C/Gas 3 while you score the skin of the pork belly; it's best to use a super-sharp knife, or even a Stanley knife. Rub the skin with a small amount of oil and season with sea salt.

2. Halve the carrots lengthways and place in the middle of a large roasting tin with the celery sticks (these are here to act as a trivet for the pork). Mix the sliced onions, sage and thyme together in a large bowl and season with salt and pepper. Scatter around the carrots and celery and then pour in the apple juice.

3. Put the pork belly in the middle of your roasting tin, directly on top of the carrot and celery 'trivet'. Cook in the oven for 3 hours. Fire up the oven to 200°C/Gas 6 for the last 30 minutes of cooking time to get the crackling really crispy.

4. Remove from the oven and allow to rest for 20–25 minutes in the roasting tray before transferring the pork to a chopping board and covering loosely with foil. Discard the carrots and celery and give the onions a good stir. Carve the pork into thick slices and serve with the roasted onions.

SIRLOIN OF BEEF WITH HERBY HORSERADISH CRUST AND PROPER ROASTING GRAVY

TERRY: There's not much better in this world than a slice of lovely, pink roast beef with that little bit of heat from some spicy horseradish. Pair that with some roasties and vegetables – it's what Sundays are all about, an absolute national treasure! Our beef comes from one of my food heroes – Peter Hannan in Northern Ireland. It's truly amazing stuff, aged in a salt chamber for 35 days, which gives it the most incredible taste in the world.

SERVES 6

2kg sirloin of beef
2 carrots, roughly chopped
1 head of garlic,
    halved horizontally
2 celery sticks, roughly chopped
1 large onion, roughly chopped
1 jar of creamed horseradish
Sea salt and freshly ground
    black pepper

For the crust

200g fresh horseradish,
    peeled and roughly chopped
Bunch of fresh parsley,
    leaves picked
Bunch of fresh tarragon,
    leaves picked
8 slices of white bread
250g melted butter

For the gravy

Large glass of red wine
2 tbsp flour
Small bunch of fresh thyme
1 litre beef stock
    (shop-bought is fine)

1. Preheat the oven to 180°C/Gas 4 while you trim away about half the fat from the top of the beef joint and score the remaining fat by about 1cm. Season generously with salt and pepper. Place a large frying pan over a high heat and brown the beef on all sides. Remove the beef, then in the same pan brown your vegetables and garlic before transferring to a roasting tin.

2. Next make the crust. Blitz the horseradish in a food processor until finely chopped, then add the herbs, bread slices, melted butter and salt and pepper and blitz again.

3. Place the beef on top of the vegetables (fat side up) in the roasting tin and spoon the crust mixture over the top of the beef, firmly packing it down and keeping it as even and as tidy as possible.

Add a good splash of water to the bottom of the roasting tray and roast in the oven for 30–35 minutes for medium/medium-rare. Remove the beef from the oven and allow to rest for 15 minutes before transferring to a board while you make the gravy.

4. Place the roasting tin of vegetables over a medium heat, add the red wine and let it bubble until the liquid has reduced by half. Whisk in the flour, then add the thyme and beef stock, stirring all the time to avoid lumps. Continue to cook for a further 5 minutes, then taste and adjust the seasoning. Strain into a gravy jug and serve with the beef.

PERFECT ROAST POTATOES

GEORGE: Roast potatoes are the measure of a top-notch Sunday dinner. It's always how I judge a good roast from a great roast. For us there are two secrets: using plenty of salt when par-boiling the potatoes and using a good duck fat or beef dripping to roast them in.

SERVES 6–8

2kg Maris Piper potatoes, peeled
Good pinch of sea salt
300g duck fat, melted
1 whole head of garlic,
    broken into unpeeled cloves
    and lightly crushed
Handful of fresh thyme,
    leaves picked

1. Preheat the oven to 180°C/Gas 4 and put a roasting tin in to heat up.

2. Cut the potatoes into large, even-sized chunks and place in a large pan. Cover with cold water and season generously with sea salt. Taste the water; it should taste nice and salty, like seawater.

3. Bring to the boil and cook until the potatoes just start to soften. Drain thoroughly in a colander, shaking them around to fluff up the edges.

4. Transfer to the preheated roasting tin with the duck fat and broken up garlic and roast for about 35 minutes, or until crispy and golden, turning halfway through. Add the thyme leaves for the last 10 minutes of cooking time. Any leftover duck fat can be reserved for next time.

ROASTED SQUASH WITH GORGONZOLA AND BASIL

There are so many varieties of squash out there that no one even thinks about, yet it's always butternut that gets the limelight! Squash can be such a thing of beauty, so look for more unusual varieties. Depending on the thickness of the skin, some need peeling and others don't.

SERVES 4 AS A MAIN COURSE OR 6 AS A SIDE DISH

2kg mixed squash
Olive oil, for drizzling
Large handful of basil leaves
100g pine nuts
Zest and juice of 1 lemon
500g Gorgonzola,
    broken into chunks
Sea salt and freshly ground
    black pepper

1. Preheat the oven to 180°C/Gas 4. Peel the squash if it has a really thick skin, then halve, scoop out the seeds and cut into large, even-sized chunks.

2. Tip the squash pieces into a roasting tin and drizzle with olive oil. Season well with salt and pepper and toss to combine.

3. Roast the squash for 20 minutes, or until tender when pierced with a knife. Remove from the oven and tip into a bowl with the basil leaves, pine nuts, lemon zest and juice; mix well.

4. Serve on a large platter, scatter over the Gorgonzola chunks and let them gently melt.

PEAS WITH BACON AND LETTUCE

Known as 'petits pois à la française' in the foodie world, this is an absolute classic: simple, super-tasty and really quick to knock up. This dish doesn't need any last-minute attention – just keep it warm and you're good to go.

SERVES 4

50g butter
1 onion, chopped
2 garlic cloves, crushed
5 rashers of thick-cut
    smoked bacon, chopped
700g frozen peas
300ml chicken stock
100ml double cream
4 heads of Baby Gem lettuce,
    quartered
Salt and freshly ground
    black pepper

1. Gently melt the butter in a large ovenproof frying pan over a low-medium heat. Add the onion, garlic and bacon and cook for 5 minutes until the onion is translucent but not coloured.

2. Add the peas and chicken stock and bring to a gentle simmer before seasoning generously with salt and pepper.

3. Stir in the cream, then add the quartered lettuce. Allow to simmer for 8–10 minutes until the lettuce has wilted.

SALT-BAKED VEGETABLES

This basic recipe for a salt crust can be used on all sorts of root vegetables, such as beetroot, carrots, celeriac, or baby turnips. Salt-baking locks in all those lovely flavours and steams the vegetables in their own salty sleeping bag.

200g root vegetables per person

For the salt crust
650g rock salt
2 egg whites
2 tbsp chopped fresh rosemary

1. Preheat the oven to 180°C/Gas 4.

2. Prepare your chosen vegetables: peel celeriac and carrots and chop into large chunks. Baby beetroot and turnips can be left whole with the skin on (halve or quarter larger vegetables). Tip into a large roasting tin.

3. Mix all the ingredients for the salt crust together in a large bowl, then pack around your vegetables. Bake in the oven following the timings below:

Beetroot: 30 minutes
Carrots/parsnips: 25 minutes
Celeriac: 1 hour
Baby turnips: 25 minutes

4. Remove and discard the salt crust before serving the vegetables.

APRICOT AND PISTACHIO STUFFING

TERRY: This recipe is for my mother, who used nothing but Paxo throughout my childhood. These fruity nutty stuffing balls are the perfect accompaniment to roast lamb.

SERVES 6–8

100g dried apricots
200g butter
2 onions, diced
3 garlic cloves, crushed
10 slices of white bread
2 large handfuls of fresh parsley
100g chopped pistachios
Salt and freshly ground
    black pepper

1. Soak the apricots in a bowl of warm water for 30 minutes so that they rehydrate and plump up. Drain, then roughly chop.

2. Preheat the oven to 180°C/Gas 4. Melt the butter in a heavy-based pan over a low-medium heat and add the onions and garlic. Cook for 5 minutes, or until soft and translucent, then remove from the heat.

3. Place the bread slices and parsley in a food processor and blitz for 5 minutes on high speed until you have green breadcrumbs. Add to the onions and garlic along with the chopped apricots and pistachios. Season with salt and pepper, mix well and shape into balls about the size of a golf ball.

4. Place the stuffing balls on a greased baking tray and cook in the oven for 10–15 minutes until golden.

CAULIFLOWER CHEESE

TERRY: I had to grow to love cauliflower. It was the one vegetable that I couldn't stand and I remember it stopping me from going out to play football as a kid (as in 'you're not leaving the table until you've eaten all your vegetables'). So for years I resented cauliflower. Then I realised that if you put enough cheese on it, anything tastes great...

This is a cheat's version; instead of making a béchamel sauce, we flavour the milk by cooking the cauliflower in it then load it up with good Cheddar and some mustard. It makes a great side for Sunday lunch (roast beef, pork, lamb or chicken) or with a grilled steak.

SERVES 4–6

2 heads of cauliflower,
   broken into large florets
1 bay leaf
2 large onions, thinly sliced
2 litres full-fat milk
600g mature Cheddar, grated
1 tbsp English mustard
3 egg yolks
Salt and freshly ground
   black pepper

1. Preheat the oven to 180°C/Gas 6.

2. Place the cauliflower florets, bay leaf, onions and milk in a large pan and season with salt and pepper. Bring to the boil and cook over a medium heat until the cauliflower is just tender. Strain through a colander, reserving the cooking milk and onions, and discard the bay leaf. Allow the cauliflower to cool before placing in a casserole dish.

3. Pour the reserved milk into a pan and add the grated cheese and mustard. Place over a low-medium heat and warm until the cheese is completely melted. Remove from the heat, stir in the egg yolks and pour over the cauliflower.

4. Cook in the oven for 15 minutes until bubbling and the top starts to brown. Serve immediately.

YORKSHIRE PUDDING

TERRY: This is actually George's mum's recipe and every time we go up North we have it as a starter with some gravy. For something different it can also be served as a dessert (without the duck fat of course), with a scoop of good-quality ice cream and dusted with vanilla icing sugar.

MAKES 6

140g plain flour
4 large eggs, beaten
190ml milk
Duck fat, beef dripping
    or a splash of vegetable oil

1. Preheat the oven to 220°C/Gas 7 and put a 6-hole Yorkshire pudding tray in the oven to heat up.

2. Tip the flour into a large bowl and make a well in the centre. Add the eggs, then gradually pour in the milk, whisking until you have a thick, smooth batter.

3. Drizzle half a tablespoon of duck fat, beef dripping or vegetable oil into the base of each mould and return to the oven for 10 minutes.

4. Carefully pour the batter into the moulds and bake in the oven for 25 minutes, or until risen and golden brown. DON'T be tempted to open the oven door, as it will let the heat out and may cause the puddings to sink. Serve with sirloin of beef (see page 164).

TERRY'S CHOCOLATE ORANGE MOUSSE WITH GINGER SNAP CRUMBLE

We used to do a super-complicated version of this at our pop-up, which we would never attempt to do at home; it's just too much faffing around. We've simplified the recipe to make it a bit more straightforward, but it's still a cracker of a dessert. The spicy ginger snaps give a great crunch and balance out the velvety richness of the chocolate. Serve this either in lovely individual glasses for elegant dinner portions, or, as we often do, in a large serving bowl with a handful of spoons.

SERVES 8–10

For the ginger snaps
350g plain flour
2 tsp ground ginger
1 tsp bicarbonate of soda
90g chilled butter, diced
1 egg
3 tbsp golden syrup
175g soft light brown sugar

For the mousse
18 egg whites
300g good-quality dark
    chocolate (minimum
    70% cocoa solids)
180g unsalted butter
12 egg yolks
Zest of 2 oranges

Fresh mint leaves, to decorate

1. Preheat the oven to 180°C/Gas 4 and line 2 or 3 baking trays with parchment paper.

2. First make the ginger snaps. Combine the flour, ground ginger and bicarbonate of soda in a large bowl and add the diced butter. Use your fingertips to rub in until the mixture resembles fine breadcrumbs.

3. Mix together the egg, golden syrup and brown sugar in a separate bowl, then add to the flour mixture and combine until you have a firm dough. Place in the fridge to chill for 30 minutes.

4. Turn on to a lightly floured surface and roll out to a thickness of 1cm. Cut out biscuits using a round cutter (you should get about 40) and place on the lined baking trays. Bake for 7–10 minutes, or until golden brown (watch them carefully, as they can burn easily). Remove from the oven and transfer to a wire rack to cool while you make the mousse.

5. Use a hand-held electric whisk to beat the egg whites in an extra-large clean bowl until stiff peaks form. Break the chocolate into pieces and place in a heatproof bowl with the butter. Melt gently in the microwave, in 30-second bursts to avoid burning. When the chocolate and butter are melted, stir together, then whisk in the egg yolks until completely combined.

6. Gently fold the egg whites into the chocolate, adding the orange zest halfway through. Take care not to knock out too much air so it stays light and airy. Transfer to a serving bowl or individual glass dishes and chill until needed.

7. Once the biscuits have cooled completely, roughly chop them and top your mousse. Finish with some fresh torn mint leaves to add a little freshness and colour.

ROASTED PLUMS WITH PECAN NUT CRUMBLE

The key to this simple, sweet dish is making sure that when you serve it, the pecan crumble is sitting on top of the roasted plums. This ensures it stays crunchy while the plums sit in their delicious, thyme-scented roasting juices.

SERVES 4

For the plums
3 thyme sprigs
1 vanilla pod, slit lengthways
8 ripe plums, halved and
     stones removed
3 tbsp light demerara sugar

For the crumble
120g plain flour
80g sugar
80g butter
2 tbsp chopped pecans

1. Preheat the oven to 180°C/ Gas 4 and line a baking tray with parchment paper.

2. First make the crumble by mixing together the flour and sugar and rubbing in the butter with your fingertips. Stir in the chopped pecans, then spread the crumble mix over the lined baking tray to a depth of about 1cm. Bake in the oven for 15–20 minutes, then use a fork to break the mixture into small chunks. Return to the oven for a further 6–8 minutes until crunchy and golden brown in colour. Set aside and lower the oven temperature to 160°C/Gas 3.

3. Spread the thyme sprigs and split vanilla pod evenly over the base of a large roasting tin and arrange the 16 plum halves skin side down on top. Pour in 500ml of water and sprinkle the sugar over the plums.

4. Roast in the oven for 25–30 minutes until the plums are soft to the touch but still holding their shape. Set aside to cool, spooning the plum roasting juices over them every 5 minutes or so.

5. These are best served at room temperature: place 4 halves per person in a shallow bowl with a few spoonfuls of the roasting juices, then top with a generous amount of crumble on top of each plum. Serve with custard or cream.

SUNDAY DRINKING

TERRY: Sundays are all about roasting meats and drinking wine. It's the perfect day to stay at home with an old movie on the TV in the background and leisurely cooking with a spoon in one hand and a glass of your favourite wine in the other... I always add a glass of wine to my gravy and, as Keith Floyd used to say, 'If it isn't good enough to drink, it isn't good enough to cook with.'

This is a very casual guide to the wines that we think go well with roasts. Ultimately it's about what takes your fancy – here's what takes ours...

ROAST BEEF

We love a bold red wine to pair with lovely pink roast beef, such as Rioja, Barolo or Bordeaux.

ROAST PORK

Crisp, dry whites and younger reds works really well with the sweetness of pork: try a German Riesling or a Pinot Noir.

ROAST LAMB

Try a Rioja or Cabernet Sauvignon to accompany the lovely richness of this meat.

ROAST CHICKEN

A beautifully simple roast chicken can take most wine. A Chilean Sauvignon Blanc or Sancerre are perfectly crisp, especially when served super cold.

CURRIED CAULIFLOWER AND ALMOND SOUP

LINCOLNSHIRE POACHER FONDUE

WALNUT AND POTATO DUMPLINGS WITH RAINBOW CHARD
AND BERKSWELL

ROASTED ONION TARTE TATIN WITH SAGE AND BLACK PEPPER CREAM

CREAMED SPELT WITH SOFT-BOILED DUCK EGGS AND BROAD BEANS

THINGS ON TOAST

CHOCOLATE AND PEA TART

BUTTERNUT SQUASH DOUGHNUTS WITH MAPLE SYRUP
AND PISTACHIO NUTS

PEANUT WHITE RUSSIANS

VEGETABLES! In all their glory they are some of the most amazing things Mother Nature has given us – the shapes, sizes and vibrant colours of these gifts from the ground... you just can't live without them. The recipes we're sharing with you here all use familiar ingredients, some of which you've probably got knocking about in your fridge already. We want to show you how easy it is to create an incredible meat-free meal for your friends.

In this section, we celebrate some great vegetables that often play second fiddle to fish or meat... dishes like roasted onion tarte Tatin with sage and black pepper cream, a steaming bowl of curried cauliflower and almond soup, and of course... a chocolate and pea tart!

POP-UP EVENT
VEGUCATION

WHY NOT TRY...
Certain flavours work brilliantly together, such as beetroot and butternut squash, which can be roasted and served as a salad with lamb's lettuce and some crumbly blue cheese, or used to top a creamy risotto with some toasted almonds. Think about the colour combinations and how they'll look on the plate too.

TERRY: A lot of the previous pop-ups we'd put together had been focused around meat and fish. When we opened up our a la carte restaurant The Pearl in Hoxton Square, East London we really wanted to give vegetables more of a leading role. I remember sitting in a friend's garden one summer, an ice-cold beer in one hand and a plate of ripe just-picked tomatoes, a hunk of crumbly Cheddar and bread in the other and thinking, 'This is the most delicious thing I've ever eaten!' Inspired by the memory of that simple but incredible lunch I'd shared with a friend, we wanted to create a menu of sharing plates where top quality, seasonal vegetables were the star of the show. Some of the dishes we created included a velouté of broad beans with spiced pea fritters, a beautifully vibrant plate full of fresh flavours. We also had a baked tomato dish with goats' curd, Welsh rarebit and basil – a great combination of tangy, sweet and creamy.

GEORGE: We were changing the menu almost every day and using as many seasonal vegetables as we could. This was a fantastic lesson for me in terms of learning how to marry different flavours together, such as walnut and potato dumplings with salty cheese. It also taught me about the importance of balance in the sharing dishes on our menu. One of my favourite dishes was so simple but really delicious – heritage radishes with fennel mayonnaise.

There are only so many vegetable-related songs in existence that are good enough to keep you dancing.

For our pop-up event The Beach Boys and Marvin Gaye certainly came up trumps! I know we included a Meatloaf song at a veg pop-up... but it's just a cracking tune.

20p 50p £1 £2

You can find a link to this playlist at
checkonpresents.co.uk

VEGETABLES
THE BEACH BOYS

STARMAN
DAVID BOWIE

THE ONION SONG
MARVIN GAYE

THIS MUST BE THE PLACE (NAIVE MELODY)
TALKING HEADS

LET'S CALL THE WHOLE THING OFF
FRED ASTAIRE

SUNDAY MORNING
VELVET UNDERGROUND

★ PLAYLIST ★

PARADISE BY THE DASHBOARD LIGHT
MEAT LOAF

YOUR COVER'S BLOWN
BELLE AND SEBASTIAN

THE GOOD LIFE
TONY BENNETT

ME AND JULIO DOWN BY THE SCHOOLYARD
PAUL SIMON

ANOTHER ONE BITES THE DUST
QUEEN

ONE OF THESE THINGS FIRST
NICK DRAKE

CURRIED CAULIFLOWER AND ALMOND SOUP

The flavours of cauliflower and curry are great together, while the nutty almonds round this silky soup off perfectly, with a burst of sweetness coming from the golden raisins.

SERVES 4

50g butter
1 tbsp groundnut oil
100g shallots, chopped
1 head of cauliflower,
    broken into small florets
1 tbsp Madras curry powder
100g ground almonds
500ml full-fat milk
Handful of toasted flaked
    almonds, to garnish
Handful of golden raisins, soaked
    in warm water until plump

1. Put the butter and oil into a large pan and place over a medium heat until the butter has melted. Add the shallots and cook until translucent but not coloured.

2. Add the cauliflower to the pan, stirring to ensure that all the pieces are coated in the butter/oil. Fry gently for 5 minutes before stirring in the curry powder and ground almonds. Keep stirring as you add the milk, then reduce the heat and simmer for 5–10 minutes, until the cauliflower is cooked.

3. Blitz the soup with a hand-held stick blender until smooth. Ladle into bowls and serve piping hot, scattered with the toasted almonds and golden raisins.

LINCOLNSHIRE POACHER FONDUE

TERRY: The first time I had proper fondue was at my friend Phil's wedding in Megève, near Mont Blanc in the French Alps. We had been celebrating hard for a couple of days when about 15 of us decided to go out to the local fondue restaurant. It was absolutely great: big vats of molten cheese with lots to dip into it – the perfect 'sharing with friends' dinner. Needless to say I've always been a fan of melted stringy cheese on toast, so fondue is the dream for me. Here we use a great British cheese packed full of nutty flavour. Bring out the fondue set for a fun retro dinner party.

SERVES 6–8

50g butter
3 banana shallots,
    very finely chopped
2 garlic cloves,
    very finely chopped
500ml white wine
Juice of ½ lemon
800g Lincolnshire Poacher
    cheese, grated
200g Parmesan, grated
Grating of nutmeg
Ground white pepper
Cubes of good bread and crunchy
    baby vegetables, to serve

1. Melt the butter in a heavy-based pan over a low-medium heat and gently soften the shallots and garlic for 5 minutes.

2. Add the white wine and lemon juice and bring to the boil. Reduce the heat to low and gradually stir in both cheeses until smooth and silky. Season to taste with freshly grated nutmeg and ground white pepper.

3. Serve the fondue in the pan straight to the table so it is nice and hot. Dip with a selection of cubed bread and crunchy baby vegetables.

4. After a while the mixture will cool and set; just pop it back over a low heat and reheat, stirring gently.

WALNUT AND POTATO DUMPLINGS WITH RAINBOW CHARD AND BERKSWELL

This is our English version of classic Italian gnocchi. The walnuts give it a lovely crunch and the colours of the rainbow chard are absolutely beautiful. Combined with the salty Berkswell cheese (which is similar to Parmesan), this is posh comfort food at its best.

SERVES 4–6

500g rainbow chard
Splash of good-quality olive oil
2 shallots, finely chopped
2 garlic cloves, chopped
200g butter
1 tbsp chopped fresh parsley
100g Berkswell cheese, grated,
   plus extra shavings to serve

For the dumplings
300g floury potatoes,
   such as Maris Piper
90g plain flour
½ beaten egg
40g walnuts, finely grated
Olive oil, for drizzling
Sea salt and freshly ground
   black pepper

1. First make the dumplings. Preheat the oven to 180°C/Gas 4 and bake the potatoes in the oven for about 40 minutes, or until cooked all the way through. Allow to cool a little before cutting in half and removing the flesh. Push the potato flesh through a potato ricer and set aside to cool.

2. Mix 200g of the dry mashed potato with the flour, egg and walnuts and season with salt and pepper to make a firm dough. Roll into 2.5cm sausages and cut into bite-sized pieces around 2cm long.

3. Bring a large pan of salted water to the boil. Add the dumplings and cook for 4–5 minutes, or until they start to float to the top. Remove with a slotted spoon and transfer to a bowl of cold water to stop the cooking process. Drain and drizzle with a little olive oil, then set aside while you cook the chard.

4. Separate the chard stalks from the leaves and wash both leaves and stalks. Chop the stalks into batons. Pour a splash of olive oil into a large, heavy-based pan and gently fry the chard stalks, shallots and garlic over a medium heat until the shallots are soft, about 5 minutes. Add 200ml of water and bring to a simmer before adding the butter and parsley.

5. Add the dumplings to the pan along with the grated cheese and reheat, stirring gently. Serve on a large platter and finish with a few shavings of cheese.

You can keep the potato skins and pop them back into the oven until crisp. Great as a snack with a dip of your choice.

ROASTED ONION TARTE TATIN WITH SAGE AND BLACK PEPPER CREAM

TERRY: The smell of frying onions has got to be one of my favourites. It reminds me of those burger vans with mountains of fried onions cooking away. Don't get me wrong; this recipe is a far cry from Bob's Burger Van. A slice of this warm tart finished with a good dollop of the sage and black pepper cream is as beautiful as it is tasty.

SERVES 6–8

400g ready-made puff pastry
Splash of olive oil
1 kg baby onions, peeled
5 garlic cloves, grated
50g butter
200ml red wine
2 tbsp fresh thyme leaves
150ml vegetable stock
250g caster sugar
Salt and freshly ground
    black pepper

For the sage cream
150ml double cream
4 sage leaves, chopped
1 tsp freshly ground black pepper

1. Preheat the oven to 180°C/Gas 4 while you roll out the pastry to a thickness of 5mm on a lightly floured board.

2. Make the sage cream: whip the cream to soft peaks before adding the chopped sage and black pepper. Set aside in the fridge until needed.

3. Heat the olive oil in a large, ovenproof frying pan and fry the onions over a medium heat for about 10 minutes, or until golden brown. Add the garlic and butter and cook for a few minutes to soften before turning up the heat and adding the red wine, thyme leaves, vegetable stock and salt and pepper. Let it bubble away until the liquid has reduced by two-thirds. Add the sugar and reduce again until you have a light caramel. Allow to cool in the pan.

4. When the onions have cooled, top with a circle of puff pastry just larger all round than the top of the pan. Tuck the excess pastry in around the sides and prick the top to allow steam to escape. Cook in the oven for 15–20 minutes until golden brown on top.

5. Remove from the oven and let sit for 5 minutes before very carefully turning out on to a large plate. Serve topped with the sage cream.

CREAMED SPELT WITH SOFT-BOILED DUCK EGGS AND BROAD BEANS

This is our version of a nice little Italian risotto, but using spelt, which gives a lovely nutty flavour. We like to top it with a rich, runny-yolk duck egg, but chicken eggs work just as well.

SERVES 6

6 duck eggs
1 tbsp rapeseed oil
3 banana shallots, finely diced
2 celery sticks, finely diced
1 carrot, finely diced
3 garlic cloves, crushed
500g spelt
300ml white wine
1.5 litres hot vegetable stock
200ml crème fraîche
200g frozen broad beans,
    defrosted and outer skins
    removed
1 tbsp chopped fresh parsley
100g cold butter, diced
Salt and freshly ground
    black pepper

1. Cook the duck eggs in a pan of boiling water for 7 minutes, then drain and plunge into cold water. When cool enough to handle, carefully peel the eggs and set aside.

2. Heat the oil in a heavy-based pan and gently fry the shallots, celery, carrot and garlic for about 5–6 minutes before adding the spelt. Cook for a few minutes over a medium heat before adding the white wine. Let it bubble until the liquid has reduced by half, stirring all the time.

3. Gradually add the hot stock, stirring continuously until the spelt is cooked (this should take about 5 minutes). Add the crème fraîche, broad beans and parsley.

4. Finish by stirring in the diced butter and seasoning with salt and pepper. Serve on a large platter with the duck eggs on top.

THINGS ON TOAST

Most things in the world taste great with a lovely grilled bit of bread
underneath. Here are a few of our favourites: great for a light lunch,
a late-night snack or even cut into fingers for canapés. We use thick-cut
sourdough toast but feel free to use whatever you like... we all grew up
eating cheese on sliced white toast, right? All recipes serve 1/make 1 large
piece of toast. We've been relaxed about the quantities, as it's really about
what you've got knocking around the fridge and what takes your fancy.

CHOPPED TOMATOES WITH CHILLIES AND CHIVES

1 large, ripe tomato, chopped
½ tsp finely chopped red chilli
1 tbsp snipped chives
Splash of sherry vinegar
Pinch of sugar
Sea salt and freshly ground
    black pepper

1. Place all the ingredients in a
bowl and mix to combine.

2. Season to taste with salt and
pepper and pile on to your toast.

SMASHED AVOCADO WITH SPRING ONION AND CORIANDER

½ avocado, peeled and stoned
Juice of 1 lime
Splash of Tabasco
Thinly sliced spring onions
Fresh coriander leaves
Sea salt and freshly ground
    black pepper

1. Place the avocado in a bowl
with the lime juice, Tabasco and a
pinch of salt and pepper. Mix well,
gently crushing the avocado with
the back of a fork, before adding
the spring onions.

2. Pile on to your grilled sourdough
and top with coriander leaves.

ROASTED GARLIC WITH PARSLEY AND SHALLOTS

1 extra-large head of garlic
Drizzle of olive oil
1 banana shallot, thinly sliced
1 tbsp freshly chopped parsley,
    plus extra to garnish
Splash of sherry vinegar
Sea salt

1. Preheat the oven to 180°C/Gas 4.
Drizzle the whole head of garlic
with some olive oil and a pinch of
sea salt and wrap in foil. Bake in the
oven for about 40 minutes, or until
completely soft.

2. Put the sliced shallot, chopped
parsley and sherry vinegar into a
bowl, along with another splash of
olive oil. Season with salt and toss
to combine.

3. Let the garlic cool to room
temperature, then squeeze the
softened garlic out of the cloves.
Spread straight on to your toast
and top with the parsley and
shallot mix. Garnish with the
remaining parsley leaves. Couldn't
be easier. This is also great spread
over a steak, stirred through pasta
or used as the base for a sauce.

GRILLED COURGETTES WITH CAPERS AND BERKSWELL

1 courgette
Splash of olive oil
Few capers
Zest of ½ lemon
Finely grated Berkswell cheese
Sea salt and freshly ground
    black pepper

1. Slice the courgettes on the diagonal into 3mm thick slices and place in a bowl with the olive oil and some salt and pepper. Mix well.

2. Place a griddle pan over a medium-high heat and cook the courgettes until nicely browned on both sides, turning to get good char lines.

3. Arrange the courgette slices on your toast and top with the capers, lemon zest and a generous grating of Berkswell cheese.

CHOCOLATE AND PEA TART

The sounds like a strange combination but trust us, it really works. The pea mousse is lovely and sweet and has a super-fresh minty burst that cuts through the rich, dark chocolate. We just love the idea of using peas in a dessert, and the colour looks ace.

SERVES 10–12

1 cooked sweet pastry tart case
(see Bakewell tart, page 33)

For the mousse
4 sheets of leaf gelatine
300g frozen peas
1 bunch of mint leaves
90ml double cream
1 tbsp caster sugar

For the chocolate ganache
500ml double cream
500g dark chocolate
(minimum 70% cocoa solids)
Pinch of sea salt

1. Follow steps 1–3 of the Bakewell tart recipe on page 33 to make a sweet pastry case.

2. Soak the gelatine leaves in a small bowl of cold water for a few minutes until softened. Meanwhile bring a pan of water to the boil and add the peas and mint leaves. Cook for 1 minute, then drain, put in a food processor or blender and blitz until smooth.

3. Squeeze the excess water out of the gelatine leaves and add to the peas, along with the cream and sugar. Blend again until smooth, then pass through a fine sieve and set aside to cool.

4. Heat the cream in a heavy-based pan until just before boiling point. Remove from the heat, add the chocolate and stir until melted and smooth. Add a pinch of sea salt and stir again.

5. Pour the chocolate ganache into the cooled pastry case and allow to set for 30 minutes until firm. Top with the pea and mint mousse and transfer to the fridge to chill.

BUTTERNUT SQUASH DOUGHNUTS WITH MAPLE SYRUP AND PISTACHIO NUTS

Not many vegetables could pull off being in a doughnut, but butternut squash totally can. The maple syrup and nuts finish it off with sweetness and crunch. Perfect with a good cup of coffee.

MAKES 10–15

2 eggs
2 tbsp melted butter
50ml milk
4 tbsp sugar
4 tbsp soft light brown sugar
150g roasted and mashed
    butternut squash
1 vanilla pod, slit lengthways
    and seeds scraped out
350g plain flour,
    plus extra for dusting
1½ tsp bicarbonate of soda
1 tsp baking powder
1 tsp cream of tartar
Pinch of salt
Good pinch each of
    ground nutmeg, cinnamon,
    ginger and allspice
Vegetable oil, for frying

To serve
Icing sugar, for dusting
Maple syrup
Chopped pistachios

1. Put the eggs, butter, milk, sugars, butternut squash and vanilla seeds in a large bowl and mix until well combined. Whisk together the remaining dry ingredients in a separate bowl.

2. Add the dry ingredients to the wet mixture and stir until thoroughly combined – the dough will be very soft and sticky. Cover the bowl with cling film and chill in the fridge for at least 2 hours.

3. Turn the dough out onto a heavily floured surface and use floured hands to shape it into golf-ball-sized pieces. Don't worry too much about the shape of the pieces; they'll puff up as they cook.

4. Heat the oil in a large, heavy-based pan until it reaches 180°C (use a kitchen thermometer or drop a tiny piece of dough into the oil; if it sizzles immediately the oil is hot enough). Deep-fry the doughnuts in small batches of four or five until golden brown, turning them over halfway through cooking. Remove with a slotted spoon and drain on kitchen paper.

5. Dust the doughnuts with icing sugar while still warm, drizzle with maple syrup and scatter chopped pistachios over the top.

PEANUT WHITE RUSSIANS

This pays homage to one of our all-time favourite film characters, a little nod to 'The Dude' in The Big Lebowski. *The white Russians were his signature drink!*

MAKES 4

2 tbsp smooth peanut butter
200ml milk
100ml good-quality vodka
100ml Kahlúa (coffee liqueur)
Ice
Toasted peanuts, to decorate

1. Place the first four ingredients in a cocktail shaker over ice and gently shake for about 30 seconds.

2. Strain into tumblers filled with ice. Serve with some lightly toasted peanuts scattered over the top.

DUCK ON TOASTED RYE BREAD WITH CRANBERRY SAUCE
AND CHOPPED PISTACHIOS

VEGETABLE LEAVES

BLACK TREACLE AND FENNEL-CURED SALMON

HAY-BAKED HAM WITH PALE ALE SAUCE

CRISPY SPROUTS WITH BACON DRESSING

ROAST TURKEY AND CRANBERRY SAUCE

ROAST PARSNIPS AND APPLES WITH DRY-ROASTED WALNUTS

BOXING DAY PANCAKES WITH WARM BRANDY CUSTARD

WHISKEY MINCE PIES

MULLED CIDER WITH CALVADOS

It's the most wonderful time of the year... Christmas holidays around the world bring people together to watch bad television and have arguments over who's cheating at board games. The festive season is very much about food and family. Our recipes for crispy sprouts with bacon, duck on toasted rye bread and the best way to eat Christmas pudding – Boxing Day pancakes with brandy custard – will do the trick.

We've created a versatile menu of dishes in this chapter – whether you're throwing a New Year's Eve party and want to offer canapé-style bites to go with a lovely mulled cider or champagne cocktail, or whether you're going all out for a traditional Christmas lunch with all the trimmings.

POP-UP EVENT
FESTIVE FEASTS

WHY NOT TRY...

If you've got a big crowd to feed over the festive period the key thing is not to be shy about asking them to pitch in and help! We always get our families to set the table if we're busy in the kitchen preparing a meal for lots of people. Or, get someone to peel the spuds at the table while you crack on with preparing the turkey. Friends and family will always want to help out and it puts them at ease if you give them a job to do!

TERRY: Christmas for me is summed up by the movie *Santa Claus* with Dudley Moore, *Only Fools and Horses*, eating dozens and dozens of pigs in blankets, going to my Nan's house and not cooking dinner. I leave it to my relatives, put my feet up for the day and try to stay out the way before I annoy my mum and nan by sticking my oar in… more often than not they will give me a slap round the ear and tell me to get out of the kitchen. It doesn't matter how old you get, your parents will always treat you like a kid at Christmas! Before Check On was even born, George and I decided to knock up a load of whiskey mince pies (we've included the recipe in this chapter for you), which we took to one of George's club nights years ago. People loved them and in a way it sowed the seed of what was to come for us and our food venture.

GEORGE: In my family we have been eating fillet steak and chips on Christmas Day for the last five years. The dogs always eat well over Christmas – everyone's a winner. I always lose at Monopoly but always win at being the most merry. I love the festive period because it's the time of the year when my whole family come together for a few days and just kick back, catch up and relax. The rest of the year often feels like such a whirlwind and we're often never all in the same place at the same time. I know for some of our friends, Christmas can be a difficult time with family, so Terry and I always throw a pre-Christmas festive feast for our friends. We spend the afternoon sharing a meal together and getting tipsy before everyone goes their separate ways for the holidays – for us it's a great way to kick off the Christmas break. To really get you in the festive mood, stick on our Christmas playlist, dust off the karaoke machine and have a good singalong. MERRY CHRISTMAS!

20p 50p £1 £2

You can find a link to this playlist at
checkonpresents.co.uk

WHITE CHRISTMAS
★ **BING CROSBY** ★

FAIRYTALE OF NEW YORK
☆ **THE POGUES** ☆

MERRY CHRISTMAS
(I DON'T WANT TO FIGHT TONIGHT)
☆ **THE RAMONES** ☆

SANTA BABY
★ **EARTHA KITT** ★

MERRY XMAS EVERYBODY
★ **SLADE** ★

LAST CHRISTMAS
☆ **WHAM!** ☆

PLAYLIST

JINGLE BELL ROCK
☆ **BOBBY HELMS** ☆

HAVE YOURSELF A MERRY LITTLE CHRISTMAS
★ **FRANK SINATRA** ★

THE CHRISTMAS SONG
★ **NAT KING COLE** ★

ALL I WANT FOR CHRISTMAS IS YOU
☆ **MARIAH CAREY** ☆

FROSTY THE SNOWMAN
☆ **GENE AUTRY** ☆

CHRISTMAS WRAPPING
★ **THE WAITRESSES** ★

DUCK ON TOASTED RYE BREAD WITH CRANBERRY SAUCE AND CHOPPED PISTACHIOS

We like to serve these as a canapé on finger-sized slices of toasted rye bread but they also make a lovely warm starter. You can use shop-bought cranberry sauce or follow our easy recipe for homemade cranberry sauce on page 217.

SERVES 10

3 duck breasts
½ tsp fresh thyme leaves
6 juniper berries,
    crushed and finely chopped
Zest of 1 orange
Splash of rapeseed oil
Sliced rye bread
1–2 tbsp cranberry sauce
1 tsp pistachios, chopped
Sea salt and freshly ground
    black pepper

1. Use a very sharp knife to score the skin of the duck.

2. Pop the breasts into an airtight plastic container with the thyme leaves, juniper berries, orange zest, rapeseed oil and salt and pepper. Mix well and allow to sit for 40 minutes.

3. Place a frying pan over a medium heat and add the duck breasts, skin side down. Cook for 5 minutes on each side for a nice medium rare before removing and allowing to rest.

4. While the duck is resting, toast the rye bread and cut into strips or rectangles. Slice your duck breast into 5mm strips and season with salt and pepper. Spread cranberry sauce on your rye toast and top with slices of duck. Finish with chopped pistachios and serve either as individual canapés or with a few salad leaves as a starter.

VEGETABLE LEAVES

This is a lovely, fresh vegetarian canapé. It's such a clean-tasting bite, bursting with flavour, plus it looks absolutely beautiful, which always helps.

MAKES 10

20g butter
70g frozen peas, defrosted
4 fresh mint leaves
10 medium-sized inner
    Baby Gem leaves
1 carrot, finely diced
1 candy beetroot, finely diced
2 long radishes, finely sliced
1 tbsp Quick Vinaigrette
    (see page 148)
Handful of coriander cress
Sea salt and freshly ground
    black pepper

1. Melt the butter in a pan over a low heat and add the peas, mint leaves and salt and pepper. Warm through for a minute or two, then transfer to a food processor or blender and blitz to a purée (try to get it as smooth as possible). Allow to cool.

2. Arrange the Baby Gem leaves on a plate and spread a teaspoon of the pea purée on each one.

3. Dress the carrot, beetroot and radishes with the vinaigrette and season with more salt and pepper, to taste. Drizzle the mixture across the lettuce leaves and finish by scattering over some coriander cress.

BLACK TREACLE AND FENNEL-CURED SALMON

This recipe needs to be prepared 2 days in advance but the results are well worth the wait: it's a great special occasion dish. When you cut through that dark outer layer to reveal the beautiful orange of the salmon you will fall in love with it.

SERVES 10

70g black treacle
1 tsp fennel seeds
35g sea salt
Zest of 1 orange
1 tsp freshly ground black pepper
500g whole salmon fillet,
    pin-boned and trimmed of fat
1 fennel bulb, very finely sliced

1. Lightly warm the treacle over a bowl of hot water and mix with the fennel seeds, sea salt, orange zest and black pepper.

2. Lay the salmon skin side down on a large sheet of cling film and brush the top all over with the treacle mixture. Pack the sliced fennel on top, then wrap the fish tightly in about 4 layers of cling film. Transfer to a dish and place in the fridge for 2 days.

3. After 2 days remove the cling film, wipe away the marinade and discard the sliced fennel. Pat the salmon dry with kitchen paper before slicing; you can slice this as thin as you like or, as we do, cut into 5mm slices, roll into spirals and secure with a cocktail stick.

HAY-BAKED HAM WITH PALE ALE SAUCE

Before you start this recipe you need to pop to your local pet shop and pick up some hay. Baking in hay gives such a unique flavour. It sounds very 'cheffy' but it's actually super easy. The roasting juices from this are soooo good and make an excellent sauce. Any leftovers won't last long, we promise. This is the kind of show-stopping dish that you can serve up at a festive gathering of any kind.

SERVES 4–6

For the ham
Large handful of hay
900ml pale ale
Handful of fresh rosemary sprigs
Handful of fresh thyme sprigs
1 boneless ham joint, about 2kg

For the sauce
300ml pale ale
Ham roasting juices
100g butter
1 tbsp flour
1 tsp wholegrain mustard
Sea salt and freshly ground black pepper

1. First soak the hay: put it in a shallow bowl and pour over the pale ale. Leave for at least 3 hours.

2. Preheat the oven to 180°C/Gas 4. Remove about half the hay from the ale and in a large casserole dish, mix with the rosemary and thyme sprigs. Spread out in an even layer. Place the ham joint on top, skin side up, then top with the remaining hay.

3. Pour over the ale that is left, pop the lid on and bake in the oven for 2 hours, removing the lid for the last 30 minutes. Remove from the oven and allow to rest in the dish for 20 minutes before removing the ham joint.

4. Meanwhile make the sauce. Strain the roasting juices through a sieve into a pan and add the pale ale. Place over a medium heat and bubble until the liquid has reduced by one-third.

5. Melt the butter in a separate pan and add the flour. Cook over a medium heat for 2–3 minutes, stirring. Gradually add the hot ale and ham stock, whisking all the time to avoid lumps. Add the mustard and season with salt and pepper (you may not need much salt as the ham will be quite salty).

6. Allow the ham to cool before slicing and serving. This goes down a treat for an old-school dinner with some Jersey Royal potatoes and minted peas.

CRISPY SPROUTS WITH BACON DRESSING

Poor old Brussels sprouts. In the UK they're relegated to just four days a year in December, whereas they love them over the other side of the pond. They were on every menu in every place we went to when we popped up in LA! The salty gems of bacon and fried sprouts are a perfect combination.

SERVES 6

1 litre vegetable oil
600g Brussels sprouts, halved
100g Bacon Butter (see page 136)
2 tbsp red wine vinegar
Sea salt and freshly ground
  black pepper

1. Heat the vegetable oil in a large, heavy-based pan to 180°C (drop a cube of bread into the oil to test the temperature; it should sizzle and turn golden).

2. Deep-fry the Brussels sprouts in batches for 3–5 minutes, until crispy on the outside and crunchy on the inside. Transfer to a plate lined with kitchen paper to absorb any excess oil and season with salt and pepper while you cook the rest.

3. Melt the bacon butter in a large frying pan over a medium heat and add the sprouts. Toss in the butter until coated, then add the red wine vinegar and stir well. Serve immediately.

ROAST TURKEY AND CRANBERRY SAUCE

A lot of people are intimidated by the size of their turkey and overcook it, but the best way to approach it is to think of it as just a big chicken. Slashing the legs will allow them to cook at the same time as the breast. Take your turkey out of the fridge at least an hour before roasting to allow it to come up to room temperature.

Our tip for great turkey is to baste the bird with the roasting juices every 15 minutes. It is hard work but definitely worth doing for the last 30 minutes of cooking time.

SERVES 6–8

2 carrots, roughly chopped
2 celery sticks, roughly chopped
2 onions, roughly chopped
1 whole garlic bulb,
    split horizontally
3kg free-range turkey
2 lemons, halved
Salt and freshly ground
    black pepper

For the cranberry sauce
1kg frozen cranberries
200g caster sugar
4 cinnamon sticks
1 tbsp ground allspice

1. Preheat the oven to 180°C/Gas 4.

2. Arrange the carrots, celery, onions and garlic over the bottom of a large roasting tin and place the turkey on top.

3. Make slashes in the legs and thighs (this will help the leg meat cook at the same time as the breast meat) and place the lemon halves inside the cavity of the bird. Season well with salt and pepper.

4. Add a splash of water (to prevent the roasting juices from evaporating) and roast in the oven for 1¾–2 hours, basting the turkey with the roasting juices every 15 minutes if you can.

5. When the skin is nice and crispy and the juices run clear when the thickest part of the thigh is pierced with a knife, take out of the oven and leave to rest for 30 minutes.

6. While the turkey is cooking make the cranberry sauce. Place all the ingredients in a heavy-based pan and bring to the boil. Reduce the heat and allow to simmer for 20–30 minutes. Remove the cinnamon sticks before serving.

ROAST PARSNIPS AND APPLES WITH DRY-ROASTED WALNUTS

TERRY: Roast parsnips are a must on a Sunday or for a festive dinner. I always cut them lengthways; that way they are fat and sweet at one end and pointy and crispy at the other. This is another vegetable that I never bother to peel – there's so much flavour in the skin it's a pity to lose it. The same goes for the apples.

SERVES 4–6

3 parsnips, quartered lengthways
3 Granny Smith apples,
    quartered and cored
1 tbsp rapeseed oil
1 tbsp dried oregano
Sea salt

For the dry-roasted nuts
200g walnuts
½ tsp freshly ground
    black pepper
1 tsp ground cumin
1 tsp smoked paprika
½ tsp sea salt
½ tsp caster sugar

1. Preheat the oven to 180°C/Gas 4.

2. Place all the ingredients for the dry-roasted nuts in a large bowl and mix together. Spread out on a non-stick baking tray and roast in the oven for 15 minutes, giving the tray a shake halfway through, until golden brown. Set aside.

3. Place the quartered parsnips and apples in a bowl and add the rapeseed oil, oregano and salt to taste. Mix well before tipping into a roasting tin. Roast in the oven for 20–30 minutes, or until the parsnips are cooked.

4. Serve the parsnips and apples with the walnuts scattered over the top.

BOXING DAY PANCAKES WITH WARM BRANDY CUSTARD

TERRY: Here we use leftover Christmas pudding for a great fruity pancake mix. Christmas pudding lasts for ages, so this doesn't have to be confined just to Boxing Day. I came up with this one year as a breakfast dish (but without the custard) – we'd used up all the bacon and sausages for pigs in blankets, a very forgivable offence in my eyes. We've added some boozy custard to make this version into a real treat dessert.

If you just want plain pancakes, leave out the Christmas pudding and add a tablespoon of sugar to the mix.

SERVES 2

230g plain flour
1 tbsp baking powder
2 large eggs
300ml full-fat milk
Butter, for frying
200g Christmas pudding, finely crumbled

For the brandy custard
100ml full-fat milk
200ml double cream
4 egg yolks
1 tbsp caster sugar
50ml brandy

1. Preheat the oven to its lowest setting to keep your pancakes warm. Pop the flour, baking powder, eggs, and milk into a food processor or blender and blitz until smooth. Set aside to rest for 20 minutes to let the baking powder do its thing.

2. Melt a knob of butter in a heavy-based frying pan over a medium heat until gently bubbling. Meanwhile add the crumbled Christmas pudding to the pancake batter and mix well.

3. Add a ladle of the batter to the pan and swirl to coat the surface. Cook for a few minutes until the top starts to set and you can see bubbles appearing. Turn carefully and cook the other side for another minute. Keep warm in the oven while you cook the rest and prepare the custard.

4. Gently heat the milk and cream in a small pan over a low-medium heat. Whisk the egg yolks and sugar together in a separate bowl until thick. Slowly pour the warm milk and cream into the egg mix, whisking all the time. Return to the pan and gently cook until thick enough to coat the back of a spoon, whisking continuously. Add the brandy and set aside until ready to serve.

5. When you are ready to serve, pile the pancakes high and pour over the brandy custard.

WHISKEY MINCE PIES

TERRY: I first made these way back before we started Check On for one of George's nights in Camden Town. It was the Christmas party, so we made a big pan of mulled cider and loads of these boozy mince pies. They went down a real treat!

MAKES 10–12

50g sultanas
100ml bourbon whiskey,
    plus extra for drizzling
1 x 280g jar mincemeat
Icing sugar, to decorate

For the shortcrust pastry
130g plain flour
Pinch of table salt
55g chilled butter, diced
35ml cold water

1. Start by soaking the sultanas in the bourbon for at least 1 hour, then stir into the mincemeat and set aside for about 30 minutes.

2. To make the pastry, place the flour and salt in a bowl and rub in the butter with your fingers until you have a crumb-like mixture. Stir in the cold water and bring together to make a firm dough. Knead for a few minutes, then wrap in cling film and chill in the fridge for 30 minutes. Preheat the oven to 180°C/Gas 4 and lightly grease a 12-hole muffin tin or silicone tart tray.

3. Roll out the pastry on a lightly floured surface to a thickness of 2–3mm. Cut out 12 pastry circles, about 10cm in diameter. (If you don't have a pastry cutter use a coffee cup.) Line the tin or tray with the pastry rounds.

4. Place a generous teaspoon of the filling into each tart and bake for 15–20 minutes. Allow to cool completely before removing from the tray.

5. Drizzle a little whiskey on top of each pie and dust with icing sugar to serve.

MULLED CIDER WITH CALVADOS

This is great to greet people with as they come in from the cold – a real winter warmer.

SERVES... LOADS!

3 red apples
12 cloves
3 litres cider
Zest of 2 oranges, plus a few slices to decorate
6 cinnamon sticks
500ml Calvados

1. Stud the apples with cloves and place in a large pan. Add all the remaining ingredients and place over a low-medium heat. Simmer very gently for 30 minutes – DO NOT BOIL!

2. Serve the mulled cider in glasses with some fresh orange slices.

ULTIMATE TURKEY SANDWICH

FRIDGE SLAW

CHICKEN CURRY

CHEESE AND MARMITE TWISTY THINGS

BUBBLE AND SQUEAK CAKES

PIGGY CROQUETTES WITH TOFFEE APPLE SAUCE

SPARE EGGS

BANANA AND CHOCOLATE SOUFFLÉS

So it's the end of the week. You open the fridge and it's full of odds and ends you're not quite sure what to do with. We want to show you that you can actually create some pretty amazing meals with leftovers. We've turned a Sunday roast into bubble and squeak cakes for tea the next day and some brown bananas are transformed with a bit of love into show-stopping soufflés. There's something really satisfying – and of course economical – about making a lovely meal out of leftovers. It can often push you to use your imagination and try new ideas, giving you a new 'go to' dish to whip up mid-week. There's no reason why you can't give family and friends a leftover meal too... for example, who doesn't have heaps of turkey left over from Christmas lunch? Turning that into an incredible pie or curry works a treat.

WASTE NOT, WANT NOT

WHY NOT TRY...

We always save old jars and use them for everything from spices, flowers or cutlery, as well as making and storing homemade dressings. If you've made a trip to the fishmongers, even if they've filleted the fish for you, take home all the trimmings and make a lovely rich fish soup or stock.

TERRY: This chapter was born out of the fact that whenever we'd do a pop-up, we'd often have food left over – whether it was potato skins, some spring greens or a kilo of chicken wings! We'd always figure out a way to use everything up so that nothing went to waste. There are also those leftovers that are so delicious, you find yourself stumbling in from a night out and dipping into the fridge – tearing off strips of cold roast chicken or 'tidying up' a slice of Bakewell tart. Having a fridge full of leftovers that friends and family can help themselves to is what it's all about. I can still hear my mum mock-shouting at me to get my grubby mitts out of the fridge when me and my mates came in from the footie, starving hungry.

GEORGE: I've lost count of the number of nights we'd go to the pub after work and I'd pull out a couple of chicken breasts wrapped in cling film from my bag while searching for my wallet to get drinks in for the staff. We never throw away leftovers from our pop-ups and I am definitely inspired to think more about it when I'm cooking at home. When I first made beef Wellington (see page 72) I had some puff pastry left over. I was starving waiting for the beef Wellington to cook and knocked up some cheese and Marmite twists using the puff pastry. They really hit the spot!

20p   50p   £1   £2

You can find a link to this playlist at
checkonpresents.co.uk

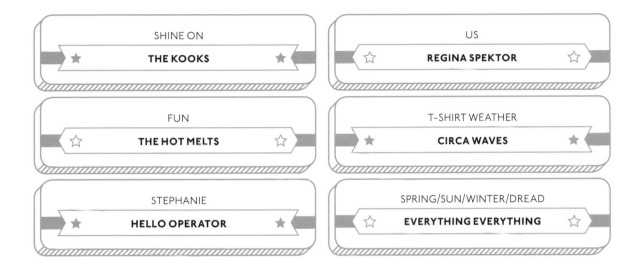

SHINE ON
THE KOOKS

US
REGINA SPEKTOR

FUN
THE HOT MELTS

T-SHIRT WEATHER
CIRCA WAVES

STEPHANIE
HELLO OPERATOR

SPRING/SUN/WINTER/DREAD
EVERYTHING EVERYTHING

PLAYLIST

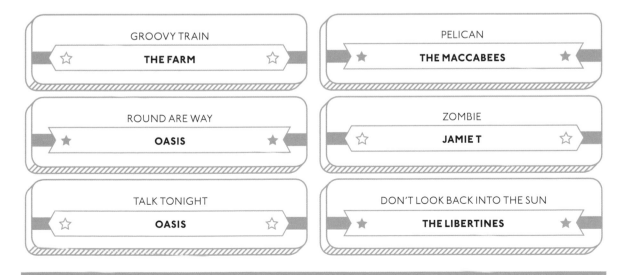

GROOVY TRAIN
THE FARM

PELICAN
THE MACCABEES

ROUND ARE WAY
OASIS

ZOMBIE
JAMIE T

TALK TONIGHT
OASIS

DON'T LOOK BACK INTO THE SUN
THE LIBERTINES

ULTIMATE TURKEY SANDWICH

Every year it goes like this: it's 4 p.m. and you can barely move after eating half a tonne of Christmas dinner... then it's 8 p.m. and you're hungry again. It's time to get creative with the leftovers!

BREAD

Use whatever you prefer; we like a nice thick-cut white loaf, toasted.

TURKEY

The key is to warm it up gently by soaking it in gravy. Place a couple of tablespoons of leftover gravy in a pan, add a few slices of turkey and heat gently for a few minutes.

BACON

Use smoked and streaky bacon, cooked until super crispy.

STUFFING

Add a few spoonfuls of stuffing to the warm gravy you used to heat the turkey slices and stir it until it's like a thick purée. Spread over the bottom slice of bread or toast.

MUSTARD MAYO

See page 47. Be generous.

BABY GEM LETTUCE

Keep it simple… add a few fresh and crispy leaves and you can't go wrong.

FRIDGE SLAW

This is a great way to use up those bits of onion, quarter of a cabbage and whatever odds and sods of vegetables you have kicking about in those plastic drawers in the bottom of your fridge. It's a great sandwich filler with some cold roast ham, perfect with any grilled meats and is always a popular staple at a summer barbecue.

Here's our recipe, but with this chapter it's all about what you have to work with.

SERVES 4

1 red onion, finely sliced
¼ white cabbage, finely sliced
1 large carrot, grated
½ fennel bulb, finely sliced
½ tsp toasted cumin seeds
1 apple, cut into matchsticks
1 tsp soft green herbs, such as
   chervil, parsley or tarragon
Juice of ½ lemon
2 tsp mayonnaise (from a jar
   or see page 46)
Salt and freshly ground
   black pepper

1. Mix all the ingredients except the mayonnaise in a large bowl until well combined.

2. Stir in the mayonnaise, season to taste with salt and pepper and mix well.

CHICKEN CURRY

Let's face it: curry is very much part of our food heritage and will be for a long, long time. We absolutely love Indian food and the amazing culture the community brings to each city across the UK. This recipe is very versatile. You can substitute the chicken and stock with almost anything. Cauliflower and king prawn is a favourite, and butternut squash and leftover slow-roasted lamb with some mint leaves is a killer combo as well.

SERVES 4-6

Vegetable oil, for frying
1 onion, finely chopped
3 garlic cloves,
    very finely chopped
1 tbsp very finely chopped
    fresh ginger
2 tsp ground coriander
1 tsp ground cumin
1 tsp garam masala
1/2 tsp ground cardamom
1/2 tsp ground cinnamon
1/2 tsp ground turmeric
1/2 tsp chilli powder (or to taste)
600g roast chicken,
    roughly flaked
1 x 400g tin chopped tomatoes
300ml chicken stock
100ml coconut milk
Bunch of fresh coriander,
    leaves chopped
Sea salt and freshly ground
    black pepper

1. Heat a splash of vegetable oil in a large, heavy-based pan and gently fry the onion, garlic and ginger over a medium heat until soft, about 5 minutes.

2. Add all the ground spices and continue to cook, stirring well to combine, for a few minutes. Add the flaked chicken, tomatoes and chicken stock.

3. Lower the heat and simmer for 30 minutes until the sauce is thick and slightly reduced. Taste and adjust the seasoning if needed.

4. Take off the heat and stir in the coconut milk and chopped coriander. Serve with some fluffy white rice and lime wedges to squeeze over.

CHEESE AND MARMITE TWISTY THINGS

This is a great little recipe for using up scraps of puff pastry you might have after making a beef Wellington or a chicken pie (see pages 72 and 50). These little delights keep hunger at bay while you're waiting for the main event. This is a very loose recipe – you can use whatever cheese you have knocking around in your fridge.

Leftover puff pastry trimmings
Marmite (warm the jar in hot
	water to loosen the contents)
Any cheese in your fridge, finely
	grated (Parmesan and Gruyère
	work well)

1. Preheat the oven to 180°C/Gas 4.

2. Gather together your puff pastry trimmings and lay them on top of each other (don't be tempted to squish them into a ball, as you will lose the characteristic puff pastry layers). Roll out the pastry into a long, thin rectangle. Cut the rectangle in two so you have two long strips, about 2cm wide.

3. Brush one of the pastry strips with some warmed Marmite before topping with grated cheese. Place the other pastry strip on top of the cheese-and-Marmite-covered strip. Twist the strips three or four times and cut into lengths about 15cm long.

4. Place the strips on a non-stick baking tray and bake in the oven for about 10–15 minutes, or until golden brown.

BUBBLE AND SQUEAK CAKES

Bubble and squeak is a classic way of using up your leftover vegetables and potatoes. It's a dish that has stood the test of time and gets its name from the noise the vegetables make when frying in the pan. This is a dish that's perfect served for brunch with a couple of fried eggs on top – don't be shy with the pepper either!

This recipe is all about the seasoning. There's no weights and measures, as it's very much a recipe using whatever is left over from dinner. Make the mix and season to taste.

Selection of cooked vegetables
(e.g. cabbage, carrots, parsnips,
peas, roast potatoes, mashed
potatoes)
Worcestershire sauce
Creamed horseradish
Freshly chopped parsley
Flour, for dusting
Vegetable oil, for frying
Butter, for frying
Sea salt and freshly ground
black pepper

1. Chop or slice any larger cooked vegetables into even-sized pieces, depending on how chunky you like your bubble and squeak. Place the vegetables in a large bowl, along with a good few splashes of Worcestershire sauce, a few spoons of creamed horseradish, some chopped parsley and a good hit of salt and pepper.

2. Give everything a really, really good mix. It should be the right consistency to mould into balls roughly the size of a small fist. If you need to add a splash of water to achieve the right consistency (or better yet some leftover gravy), then go ahead.

3. Let the mix chill in the fridge for 20 minutes before shaping into patties and dusting with a little flour.

4. Place a non-stick frying pan over a medium-high heat and add a splash of vegetable oil. Fry the cakes for a couple of minutes on each side until golden brown. Finish by adding a knob of butter to the pan.

5. Serve with a good dollop of brown sauce and some fried eggs… perfect!

PIGGY CROQUETTES WITH TOFFEE APPLE SAUCE

This is a great way to use up leftover pork belly or pulled pork. The recipe below is for snack-style bites, but you can up the pork content and serve with some buttered cabbage for more of a hefty dish.

Remember those tooth-breaking toffee apples that you used to get at fairgrounds? The toffee apple sauce here works just as well with these croquettes as it does on top of a scoop of vanilla ice cream.

MAKES 10

300g cooked pork, chopped
200g cold mashed potato
Dash of Worcestershire sauce
2 tbsp freshly chopped coriander
I tsp chilli sauce
100g flour
2 eggs, beaten
100g panko breadcrumbs
Vegetable oil, for frying
Salt and freshly ground
    black pepper

For the toffee apple sauce
200g caster sugar
150g unsalted butter
50ml double cream
500g Granny Smith apples,
    peeled, cored and diced

I. Place the chopped pork, mashed potato, Worcestershire sauce, coriander and chilli sauce in a large bowl and mix thoroughly (use your hands if necessary).

2. Divide the mixture into balls the size of a golf ball (or about 50g per ball).

3. Arrange the flour, beaten eggs and breadcrumbs in three shallow bowls. Dust the croquettes with the flour, then dip in the egg and finally roll in the breadcrumbs to coat.

4. When you have coated all the croquettes, chill them in the fridge for 15 minutes.

5. Heat a generous amount of oil in a large, heavy-based pan to 180°C (a cube of bread should sizzle and turn golden immediately). Deep-fry the croquettes in batches for 4–5 minutes, or until golden brown on all sides. Drain on kitchen paper before serving.

6. Meanwhile make the sauce. Put the sugar in a heavy-based pan and place over a very low heat until it melts and turns to a golden caramel. Add 50g of the butter and then the cream, and whisk until smooth and glossy (take care, as the pan will hiss and spit when you add the butter and cream). Melt the remaining butter in a separate pan over a low heat and add the chopped apples. Cook slowly for a few minutes until soft and tender, then add to the caramel. Use a hand-held stick blender to blend to a smooth, thick sauce. Season with salt and pepper and set aside.

7. Heat a generous amount of oil in a large, heavy-based pan to 180°C (a cube of bread should sizzle and turn golden immediately). Deep-fry the croquettes in batches for 4–5 minutes, or until golden brown on all sides. Drain on kitchen paper before serving with the toffee apple sauce.

SPARE EGGS

Everyone has the odd renegade egg or two in the fridge. They are so versatile and an absolute staple of everyone's weekly shop. These little omelettes/tortillas are quick, simple and packed full of flavour – great for brunch or an afternoon snack.

How many people these recipes serve will depend on how many eggs you have, so we've been deliberately vague with quantities. When we say cheese, we're not being specific, as with leftovers it's all about what you've got in the fridge. Also, where we've suggested something like tarragon, don't worry if you don't have any in the house – you can easily swap in something like parsley if you have that instead.

CHORIZO AND CORIANDER

Sliced chorizo
Handful of coriander,
    finely chopped
Lightly beaten eggs
Freshly ground black pepper

1. Preheat the grill to high.

2. Cook the chorizo in a dry frying pan over a medium heat until crisp. Add the coriander and cook for a further 30 seconds. Add the eggs and season with pepper. Cook until just set around the edges, then finish the omelette by sliding it under the hot grill to cook the top.

SMOKED HADDOCK AND CHIVE WITH SOURED CREAM

Butter, for frying
Cooked and flaked
    smoked haddock
Finely chopped chives
Lightly beaten eggs
Soured cream
Salt and freshly ground
    black pepper

1. Preheat the grill to high.

2. Melt the butter in a frying pan over a medium heat and add the smoked haddock and chives. Cook for a few minutes before adding the beaten eggs and seasoning with salt and pepper. Cook until just set around the edges, then finish the omelette by sliding it under the hot grill to cook the top. Top with some soured cream and serve immediately.

POTATO, RED PEPPER AND PAPRIKA

Olive oil, for frying
Cooked potato, peeled and diced
Cooked red peppers
    (from a jar is fine)
Pinch of paprika
Lightly beaten eggs
Sea salt and freshly ground
    black pepper

1. Preheat the grill to high.

2. Heat a little olive oil in a frying pan, add the potatoes, peppers and paprika and fry for a couple of minutes. Add the beaten eggs and season with plenty of salt and pepper. Cook until just set around the edges, then finish the omelette by sliding it under the hot grill to cook the top.

HAM, CHEESE AND ONION

Butter, for frying
Finely diced onion
Cooked ham, chopped
Wholegrain mustard
Chopped fresh tarragon
Lightly beaten eggs
Grated cheese

1. Preheat the grill to high.

2. Melt the butter in a frying pan and add the diced onion. Fry gently until softened before adding the chopped ham, mustard and tarragon. Add the beaten eggs and season with plenty of salt and pepper before scattering over the grated cheese. Cook until just set around the edges, then finish the omelette by sliding it under the hot grill to cook the top.

BANANA AND CHOCOLATE SOUFFLÉS

This is a cracking way of using up those squidgy bananas left in the fruit bowl. Most people hear the word soufflé and think 'oh god, I can't do that!' but it's actually really easy. It's not the quickest dessert to make, but if you take your time and prepare it carefully with a bit of love, the results are well worth the effort!

SERVES 4

Melted butter, to grease
    the ramekins
Cocoa powder and icing sugar,
    for dusting
100g dark chocolate,
    finely chopped
2 ripe bananas
1 tbsp cornflour
1 tbsp water
Juice of ¼ lemon
6 egg whites
160g caster sugar

1. Preheat the oven to 200°C/Gas 6.

2. Lightly brush the insides of four individual ramekins with melted butter, then dust the insides with cocoa powder. Sprinkle the chopped chocolate over the bottom of each ramekin in an even layer.

3. To make the banana base, put the bananas in a food processor with the cornflour, water and lemon juice and blitz until you have a smooth purée.

4. In a clean bowl whisk the egg whites until soft peaks begin to form. Start adding the sugar, a tablespoon at a time, until it is all combined.

5. Take one-third of the egg white mixture and combine with the banana purée, before gently folding in the rest of the egg white mixture (you don't want to knock out too much of the air).

6. Divide this soufflé mix evenly between the ramekins and smooth the tops. Run your finger around

the top of each ramekin to neaten (this is to make sure that the mixture doesn't stick to the sides of the ramekin when trying to rise).

7. Place the ramekins on a baking tray and cook in the oven for 10–15 minutes, or until risen and golden on top. Served dusted with icing sugar and some ice cream on the side.

LEFTOVER EGG YOLKS

You'll have some egg yolks left over at the end of this recipe. They will keep in the fridge, covered, for about 3–4 days but unfortunately, unlike egg whites, you can't freeze yolks. Keep them for glazing pies such as the chicken and girolle pie (page 50) or beef Wellington (page 72). They also make a great spaghetti carbonara when stirred with crispy pancetta and grated Parmesan into hot spaghetti.

THANKS

Firstly and most importantly we would like to thank Marianne: an amazing agent, friend and angel on our shoulder who, since we met, has been the definition of supportive; she has the ability to see the future like no one else... thank you for EVERYTHING!

Claire Bord, whose tireless efforts have helped shape the book; thank you for the great hip-hop classics and the array of sweets that kept us going when we had seemingly run out of words.

All the fantastic team at Hodder – Nicky Ross and Emma Knight who 'got it' after a 25-minute meeting and decided to put their faith in us.

Alice Laurent for designing our very first book with such style and grace.

Chris & Alex at We Three Club for their great artwork.

Georgie Clarke for your patience :) and wonderful photography. An absolute pleasure to work with and such a talent. Great to have you on the bus!

Beatrice Hurst... style never goes out of fashion-darling! For your amazing prop styling and for knowing what we think before we say it, thank you for everything.

We'd like to thank all our friends and loved ones who have supported the Check On journey so far.

Special mentions and thank yous go out to everyone who helped with pop-ups, venues, supplies and generally bailed us out of trouble!

Morten Jensen
Michelle Sullivan... hi hun!
Chris 'PK' Harding
Simon and Nicola Hutchinson @ hutchcassidy
Capital Seafood
Ronnie Murray
Kevin Gratton
Graham Blower
Jimmy Craig
The Flame
Heather Garrett
Poppy Steveni
Kate Gowing
Arianne Clarke

James Clarke
Aggy Dave
Vicki Charlton
Two Tone
Andy
Jimmy Goldstone
The Ginger Pig
Solstice Food
Alice Stanners
Emma Elwick-Bates
Anna Howes
Jacob Wheldon
Sharna McMullen
Simon Williams AKA The Welsh
Wizard
Dan Market

Chris Melian
Cheila Reais
Adam Towner
Kate Rosenware
Amy Campbell
Luka Lucyan
Tom 'Burger Bear' Reaney
Louisa Copperwaite
Clemmie Corlett and Magimix
Peter Hannan
The Love Shake guys
Scott Gallagher
Leila Monks
Laura Jones
Harvey Drummond
Fran Masey O'Neill

Lewis Thorn and family
Reg Johnson
Keeno
David Moore
Phoebe Hall
Oscar Humphreys
Louis Lillywhite
Brett Barnes
Susannah Butter
Burberry
Hugh Thomas
Rudi
Liam Hart
Patty and Bun Joe
Zoe Klinck
Ellie Jarvis

INDEX

Editorial Director: Nicky Ross
Editor: Claire Bord
Copy Editor: Clare Sayer
Project Editor: Kate Miles
Design & Art Direction: Aka Alice
Photographer: Georgie Clarke
Photographer Assistant: Joe Stone
Food Styling: Terry Edwards
Food Styling Assistant: Ellie Jarvis
Props Styling: Beatrice Hurst
Props Styling Assistant: Phoebe Hall
Proof reader: Annie Lee
Indexer: Caroline Wilding

Printed and bound by Firmengruppe APPL, aprinta druck, Wemding, Germany

Hodder & Stoughton policy is to use papers that are natural, renewable and recyclable products and made from
wood grown in sustainable forests. The logging and manufacturing processes are expected to conform to the
environmental regulations of the country of origin.

Hodder & Stoughton Ltd
Carmelite House
50 Victoria Embankment
London EC4Y 0DZ
www.hodder.co.uk